D1120806

For CHANNELS, HEALERS and HELPERS

Brian Berry

Cover Art from a painting by Charlotte Johnstone
'Humpbacks Blue' ©2000
Cover Design by Nicole Caputo
Author photograph by Linda Petry
Edited by Meryl Ann Butler

And special thanks to two who helped at a critical point:
Annaleah Atkinson and Delynn Solomon

ISBN: 978-1-7364512-0-5

Published by ***ORIGINS***
6409 Glen Abbey Lane
Bradenton Florida 34202

The texts published in these chapters have been edited for length from sound recordings made by the author. Names have been changed and identifiable biographical details have simply been omitted. All the participants in these reading sessions signed the following release at the time the reading was done:

> "I understand that the information conveyed in a reading by Brian David Berry is spiritual advice. I understand that all references to diet, health, or physical symptoms will be based on a spiritual point of view. I understand that the method for obtaining this advice is fundamentally a meditation, similar to meditations I might do myself.
>
> I understand that the application of that advice is my responsibility, and I agree to hold harmless Brian David Berry and any who assist him in this process. I understand that any advice which relates to medical conditions should be checked with my physician or other health professional.
>
> I understand that it is not meant that these readings will be closely held, but instead, widely published. Of course, appropriate changes and edits will be made on publication, to preserve the privacy of the individuals who have sought the readings. I give permission for my reading to be so published."

About the Author

Brian Berry trained with Paul Solomon from 1977 through 1979, teaching Inner Light Consciousness as a Guide all over North America and Europe. His ILC really began when a Paul Solomon reading saved the life of his infant son in 1974. Dreams were his specialty in those days, and over the years, he added The Mystery School Journal, meditation of course, and in time, Akashic and Health readings.

He came to Paul's Fellowship of the Inner Light from a faculty post at Yale. In the eighties, he earned graduate degrees in school psychology and infant and toddler development, and spent 25 years in special education, much of it with children who had low-incidence handicaps in the inner cities of Connecticut and Florida.

As time seasoned his ILC he never stopped teaching, but moved from the esotericism of the 1970's toward simple wholeness through active and vigorous work in a needy world. Twenty-five years of work with children in special classes, in orphanages and shelters on three continents in partnership with his wife and their three adopted daughters, have kept his ILC growing, joyful, and up to date, not cloistered or secret. He says these days that it is a joyous and creative relationship with Source that renews his work and his life, and that is what he wants most to share.

To Contact the Author

If you wish to contact the author please write via email: brianberry2021@gmail.com The author would enjoy hearing from you about your experience in reading this book, how it has helped you, and similar topics. This book is meant to be a guide and a road map to the inner life, only one of many, of course. If you write via U.S. Mail, please include a stamp and a self-addressed envelope.

Preface

A BOOK COMPOSED FROM AKASHIC READINGS: how much introduction does such a book need in the year 2021? Edgar Cayce, the American master of the Akashic Reading, has been gone since 1945. Hundreds of books about him are well known to readers in many languages. Hundreds, perhaps thousands, of people have followed gratefully in his footsteps, not least Paul Solomon, who worked from 1972 until his death in 1994. I was his student, and he had many others. Some have produced books of their own, and I point you to some at the back of this one.

Currently, Michael Newton, Brian Weiss, Joan Grant, and Tom Sugrue among others have written books which endure. They are not identical in form but they do proceed out from the same kind of knowledge – they are based on recall of other lives and other existences, as this one is.

Books of course are not the end product of these journeys into Universal consciousness. In every case Akashic material is given to heal or aid souls who want to live more truly and more effectively in the lives they have now. We who do this work don't claim to be infallible or unique, either one. We believe in every case that we tap a higher knowledge when we do it. I only mean to encourage those who want this dimension in their lives.

So why one more book? Am I going to spell out exactly how this works, or exactly who are the entities that meet a channel eye to eye when these answers are sought? I wouldn't presume to do that. What I mean to do is bring to life the experiences and the motives of those who seek these answers. So really, I am just a reporter of soul stories, and it is soul stories that you have here. And if you are touched by any one of these, then I trust you will put this book down and enter into prayer for the souls you are reading about. I have concealed their earthly identities but the Angels can sort them out. You will bless them and bless yourself in your own seeking when you do.

CONTENTS

1 Simeon and his Reading
2 Nora
3 Aleisha
4 Maggie and Sophia, a Master Physician
5 Janet, Who Didn't Have to Come Back
6 Doris, A Long Life
7 Gloria, an Analyst
8 Baker and Ned
9 Jan Wakes Up to Fear and Dread
10 Christine
11 Chris, Whose Father Died in Viet Nam
12 Ruth and Radiation
13 Gabriela, a Healer and a New Mother
14 Wendy and the Seventh Inning Stretch
15 Anna, a Writer and a Priestess
16 Cassie, a Healer in the Mountains
17 Leora & the Spirit of Inner Light Consciousness
Afterword

Simeon and His Reading

Chapter 1

LIKE MANY ANOTHER SEEKER I SEARCHED FOR A PSYCHIC when I found myself caught up in a dark night of the soul. My infant son was dying. He had been seriously ill for ten of his eleven months, with what today is called "failure to thrive." As he neared his first birthday he was still at his birth weight. It's a situation that comes about when parents are deeply and rancorously divided, and that was true for my wife and me. I did not recognize at the time the mental illness from which she suffered, and it was years later that psychiatrists decided a name for it.

On Simeon's first birthday I was thirty and I had been at Yale for seven years, at first on staff as a photographer, and then teaching as a visiting lecturer. I lived in one of the colleges as a resident fellow with my family. That was my livelihood, and I probably would have said it was the story of my career, to the extent that a creative photographer's life can be called a career. That life was what I thought I wanted but it was not the path I had appointed before I entered this life, I believe.

In Simeon's first year I had sought diagnosis and treatment for him at Yale-New Haven Hospital, and then in the summer of 1974 at Albany Medical Center, where my wife's cousin was a physician. The pediatricians in Albany wanted to hospitalize Simeon and feed him a "challenge diet." They also wanted to limit our time with him. My wife and I disagreed sharply about this, although in hindsight the doctors were clearly right.

When severe diarrhea occurred I was told he had hours to live, and they asked me to come to the hospital on an emergency basis. Within a few hours we had foolishly signed him out against medical advice. Then with my wife and 5-year-old son I drove Simeon back to New Haven, a three-hour drive.

A year of conflict over this had told on us both. I had lost forty pounds and my kidneys were in trouble. My wife was utterly distracted and unable to attend to the simplest tasks.

At one point I collapsed in exhaustion. I was unconscious for an hour or so. During that hour I "dreamed" that an Indian guru on the bottom of the ocean told me that the answer I needed was in Virginia Beach. His hair was in a topknot, he wore silks, and his slippers had turned-up toes. And his eyes were extraordinary, compelling, so much that I trusted him instantly despite his bizarre appearance.

All I knew about Virginia Beach was what I had read about Edgar Cayce. In response to the vision -- and believing that I had no good alternative -- I dropped my wife and both boys at her parents' Connecticut home, then drove straight on to Virginia Beach.

I arrived at Edgar Cayce's organization, the Association for Research and Enlightenment, at dawn on a Sunday morning. I sat on a bench there, in a daze. The morning was foggy and surprisingly chill for a July day. I gradually became aware of a man jogging around the A.R.E. compound. He introduced himself: he was Dr. Charles Whitehouse, a chiropractor. He asked why I was there and I spilled out my whole story.

"Well, you need a reading pretty badly," he said, "But Edgar Cayce is dead. I'm the medical director here at the A.R.E. I could guide you to some readings in the files but I think this is not a time for study. Let's get you a reading. There's a new man in town and I think he's pretty good."

I said yes, of course, and the doctor sent me to a boardinghouse to get some sleep while he made arrangements. At sundown I met him at a beach house on 37th Street, and we went upstairs to a sleeping porch where half a dozen hippies were sitting expectantly. No one said much. I was given no forms or questionnaires.

A haggard man seeming to be in his mid-thirties entered the sleeping porch. He needed a shave and a haircut and he wore faded jeans and a rumpled shirt. He was Paul Solomon, a psychic from Atlanta who, apparently, could do what Edgar Cayce used to do. My heart sank when I saw him. I was running out of time, I didn't know if Simeon was still alive, and I was in the hands of this disheveled man?

He did not speak to me or to Dr. Whitehouse. He sat on a sofa and confidently recited the Lord's Prayer ... and even in my own ragged state I felt the room fill with peace.

A bearded man about my age – James Wharton, later known as Daniel Emmanuel -- asked me my name, birthdate and place of birth; and then he spoke a brief suggestion for Solomon. He then asked me for questions. I handed him the index cards I had written my questions on, and he began to query Solomon, who was clearly in a trance state.

I was spellbound. Every word Solomon spoke rang true. I had come seeking a reading like Edgar Cayce's, not really believing that this was possible. But that was happening and I could barely grasp it. Solomon's recommendations for Simeon were brief.

> "Tiny little thing. He doesn't have the facilities for assimilation. Let's give him cow's milk mixed half and half with limewater. Give him Atomidine on the usual schedule. Rub him with peanut oil twice a day, lots of massage and handling … and don't go near him when you're afraid. We'll do a check reading in a few weeks and see how he's getting on."

That was all for Simeon. But he added something for me at the end, after a long discourse on a dream of mine. He said,

> "Now directional forces for this one can come well, and do, through the dreams. Should not be left to chance, but in the entering into sleep, focus the self, the mind, on the question as would be answered, then the dream will have more meaning. That is, the dream being in answer to a specific question, will bring the interpretation the much more quickly. Use in these manners and we'll find a building. Then the answer will be clear, having asked the question, you see?"

I didn't really see. But I was overflowing with gratitude and somehow I was convinced that his recommendations would work. But how would I gain my wife's cooperation? I had no idea. I had recorded dreams for years, taking my direction from the books of Carl Jung, but my only conscious purpose had been to use those dreams to inspire more resonant photographs.

I spent the night in Doctor Whitehouse's office with the audiotape, a cassette player, and a typewriter, impelled to transcribe every word. In the morning I left the typescript in the office and left for home with the carbon copy. When I got back to Connecticut, I got the angry reception I expected, but it didn't last long, because I fainted again a few moments after I arrived.

My wife and her mother disposed of me in a bedroom, where I slept for more than forty-eight hours. During those hours they read the transcript, persuaded a pharmacist to make up the limewater, tracked down some Atomidine in a health food store, and put the reading into action. They didn't know what a reading was, and I barely knew, but they went ahead.

Miraculously, Simeon gained seven ounces in the first week, and he improved steadily after that. I believed then, and still believe, my wife and her mother and these miraculous helpers had saved his life. But the gift of this healing, spectacular though it was, did not suddenly result in harmony between the two of us.

A new life for me unfolded from this experience. I began to utilize my dreams consciously and not desperately. One door had opened and others had swung shut and I had started on a journey that led to a new world. Before long that journey led me to a Mystery School, where I would learn to do for others what Solomon had done for me.

What a Reading is: Nora

Chapter 2

PEOPLE HAVE DONE READINGS FOR THOUSANDS OF YEARS. That is, they have deliberately yielded ordinary consciousness and taken themselves into a heightened intuitive state of mind, believing they could contact and hear or see a higher consciousness. The Book of Daniel will be familiar to most readers, and that may be the most widely known example. Today the example of Edgar Cayce is widely known as well. He was a "psychic" who did thousands of readings, mostly medical, from 1910 until his death in Virginia in 1945.

Over and over his diagnoses proved to be accurate, but acceptance for his remedies was hard-won. He did many kinds of readings, not just health or medical, giving advice on problems of faith, science, and just about every field of human endeavor. His organization is still flourishing today in Virginia Beach, and virtually all of his readings are available there. To most readers, he is a modern saint, even though his personal life aside from his readings work was outwardly ordinary. From first to last he was devoted to his family and that is one of the reasons we trust him.

Emmanuel Swedenborg did many readings as well, working in Sweden from early in the eighteenth century, whose work is also preserved and widely known, at least in Europe. He was a distinguished scientist as well. It was Swedenborg who inspired Johnny Appleseed – a real man, not a folk myth – to travel about America, creating apple orchards and spreading the teachings of Swedenborg.

In modern times there have been many channels who have found fame and a great many others who are less well known. Some have come to grief or disgraced themselves and their students through their human failings. Others have clearly lost their grip on reality and provided fodder for late-night comedians. The Dalai Lama, formerly of Tibet, would be one channel who has not, and whose teachings are widely regarded around the world.

A few years after the reading from Paul Solomon did so much to save my son, I arranged through the chaplain of Yale's medical school for Paul to speak to the medical and nursing students there, in April of 1977. His talk there was memorable to say the least, and in a matter of months I followed him to Virginia Beach and became his student.

Many years passed before I took up the practice of readings myself but I have been doing them now for more than ten years. Truly I needed the instruction and the training that Paul provided to me and to others. His instruction was given in the context of a Mystery School, although from the outside his work looked much like that of any other foundation promoting self-knowledge and spiritual growth. Mystery Schools have historically been the locus of spiritual training for those who would teach, heal, or prophesy. Historically they have rarely if ever announced themselves to the world as Mystery Schools. He preferred to call his school "The School of the Prophets," a biblical reference. Paul said of himself that he was a teacher of effective life, and he despised the word "guru," but in reality (as I saw it) his methods and his organization were very like those of the gurus who came out of India in such numbers in the second half of the twentieth century. Those gurus routinely involved themselves in every detail of their students' private lives. I have not chosen that path.

Readings are intensely private, of course. In the readings included here names have been changed and identifying details not changed but simply omitted. For every reading I do, and every one included here, I have a release from the seeker who was the subject. My one aim in publishing these readings is to help those who want to wake up and walk closely and personally with the Creator.

I know that many readers will be those who feel the call to do similar work. I can only say, it's joyous but it's a long trail and one's own shadows must be met; and it is always a path that will be guided mostly from within.

Let's look closely at one reading before we generalize further. This reading is unusual in the way it lays out richly the themes that shaped a complex life.

For Nora it was an extraordinary experience and you can hear that in her responses. There are four scenes here, each from a different past life, as if each was from a movie. She understood that. She had studied enough to believe that there is really only one life, the life of the soul.

She also understood the Akashic Record to be an imperishable layer of energy about the earth wherein is recorded the events and actions of all living beings. She understood that we had set out to read her soul history from this great record, objectively and accurately, and its existence is the basis of the readings process.

And for Nora, as she listened to this reading, the details of each scene were familiar to her from her own dreams over a period of years, dreams she had barely understood when she had them. She also understood that these scenes spelled out a lesson so fundamental that it very nearly comprised the purpose of her life this time.

So how did this document come to be? Let me describe our meeting just as it really was. Nora came to the Fellowship of the Inner Light, a little metaphysical church in Virginia Beach, not her home church, but one she had visited before. The church was founded by Paul Solomon in 1974. Paul died in 1994 but the church endures. Nora came seeking a reading consultation like those described so often in the biographies of Edgar Cayce.

Nora had made an appointment with me by telephone. She came to the church on a weekday afternoon. When she arrived we talked for about five minutes, just enough for her to feel comfortable with me. She let me know that asthma was her main concern, that and a pattern of panic attacks leading to a faint whenever she visited Richmond, home to much of her family. Then we climbed stairs to an upper room used mostly for classes.

Nora was nervous and excited but not afraid. I was myself – no different in manner, language or dress than I was in hundreds of parent conferences as a school psychologist. While we were downstairs she explained to me that she had been a rigorously trained professional musician, whose career was ended by a cancer of the middle ear. The surgery for this left her with only one working ear and with a somewhat disfigured jaw as well.

Once upstairs, I settled on a sofa, and held hands with Nora and with Jill, my "conductor." The conductor of a reading takes a channel through a guided meditation prior to the reading to ensure that the Source of the readings is consistently and wisely approached. This guided meditation is spelled out in Chapter 4. With Nora, as always, I prayed out loud for a few moments before the meditation.

I don't generally record these prayers and I can't say surely what my prayer was this day. Usually I ask for the presence of the Source of my being, and of Nora's too; and I mean the Creator.

And I ask for the clarity to exclude my own opinions and emotional reactions in order to read clearly and objectively the material I will see. If I am either repulsed or too strongly attracted to the energies I encounter, errors creep in. Together we asked that I be aided to read accurately what was relevant and needed here, according to the seeker's questions. Nora was the seeker, of course, and seeker is a better word than client.

I closed my eyes and meditated for about five minutes while Jill led me mentally into a meadow, up a terraced mountain, and into a temple on the summit. My eyes remained closed throughout the reading. As we asked Nora's questions this transcript begins, made from a sound recording done on a voice recorder. You will see that once in the reading situation her feelings overflowed and she asked about what was really troubling her.

> "Jill, the conductor here: Convey to us please the Book of Life for Nora -------, born with that name on the date August ---, --------, in ---------, Virginia. Let us draw upon Records past, present, and those formed for the future, to explain the forces at work in and about this soul. Let us consider the soul's chosen purposes for this incarnation, the deep beliefs of the soul, and the abilities untapped or little used so far in this life. We will apply all of these to the lessons and the challenges of the present."
>
> Brian: Yes, we have this Record, and we've not seen another like it. It's large, it's the size that bookbinders call "folio." It is loosely bound, for a number of soul threads have been blended here, that is, a number

of gifts and issues left unfinished in other lives have been chosen here as the part to be played, sometimes one after the other, and sometimes simultaneously.

As we go along we will explain how Nora has switched from one life to another to another in this body and in this incarnation, and how the fundamental notes of each expressed and produced growth and … not harmony, but an inner *congruity* that is unusual and not apparent to most eyes. Especially at this time, just beginning to be apparent to Nora's own eyes when she studies them in a mirror.

Now that folio appears as if bound in black, thin leather. And the pages are not grouped in signatures, nor are they bound in plain sequential order. Nora has taken one lesson, then another, and then another, in bewildering progression. But the master composer who arranged this book had both a purpose in mind, and a day in mind, when the confusion would end. We are ready for questions.

The Conductor asks Nora's first question: "My life is a train wreck. How to un-wreck it? What is my life purpose?"

Brian: As just presented in symbol, Nora's life purpose was to bind no less than four separate strands into one. It's been a difficult weave, a challenging weave. But it's really only the notion that our lives have a single purpose that has made it seem so difficult, because identity in Nora's case is a rich and flowing blend of quite disparate elements.

We are seeing now a candle, and that candle is in a wooden cup attached to a music stand. And it was with such an arrangement that this soul composed music through long, dark nights in an attic apartment, playing on an instrument used by dancing masters. This was basically a fiddle with a long slender body, not having the usual fiddle shape at all.

The name of this instrument is not in this channel's vocabulary. Its virtue was that it had the range of the violin but the volume was quite slight. Thus it was advantageous to use in the dead of night when there were other tenants downstairs.

In that life, many compositions were made. While they were eventually performed, only a few were performed by others in this composer's lifetime. So in this present life, there is a feeling that "it all just may be for nothing.'"

That feeling has haunted many efforts for Nora, in which something was fashioned in her creative consciousness, and while it found expression in this life, it did not find the ideal expression that she had envisioned. So she has been inclined to think that she is a failure. But no, she has lived far less failure than she believes.

Having trouble getting this composer's name: not Schwemmer, and not Schwemmerein … Austrian, not German. These syllables just can't be had in this channel's speech. Some of those works have survived and are occasionally performed. They were Baroque in style, and typically done for quartets and small string orchestras for use in courts. Not royal courts, but the courts of dukes and duchesses and – here's a word we don't often see – in the court of a protector. Not Cromwell the Protector, but an Austrian protector named to occupy not the throne, but the full set of throne-like powers until the heir was of age to take the throne.

This was an exciting life. This was a life full of surprises. This was a life marked by great beauty that came to this composer as he conducted his compositions and those of others in lovely candle-lit halls, for audiences who were not only enthusiastic and receptive, but also educated and able to appreciate his music.

But the nature of what might be called the music business at the time was not one that encouraged the preservation of compositions. Publication was a rare event. So this soul died at a reasonable age for the time, in his early fifties, more than a little convinced that his life had simply gone up into the rafters and disappeared. But it was not so, for he did move souls, and he did change lives with his music. But their experiences were private.

As a sad remnant from this life, Nora, you have a recurring feeling that "My most beautiful parts have not been loved, nor treasured, nor preserved when they were expressed." This is not true, however. This soul has had an impress on quite a few souls. Not a vast number, but the impression was profound and lovely.

Now we see another symbol: a modest cart, whose wheels are round and solid. The scene expands and we see a cobbled street. In this cart there stands a young person, a female this time, of gentle birth, and a gentle soul. One who came to sing sweetly, truly like a lark. Her name is being given in French: "Laurele," L-A-U-R-E-L-E.

She has been raised in a happy family, sheltered, and brought through a happy childhood. She has learned to sing beautifully and accompany herself adequately on the various kinds of keyboard parlor instruments that were in use at this time. But sadly for Laurele, this is the time of the French Revolution. We see her here just short of her nineteenth birthday, and the cart is the tumbril. She is on her way to the guillotine. Not for crimes, but solely because of her birth. For her of course it's personal. She knows she has a breast full of music. She knows she has a fountain of joy that lights her personality. She can't understand why this life is going to be snuffed out violently for things she had nothing to do with.

Seen from here, Laurele left that life, though she was only a teen, having mastered and brought to life again that singing voice; and more important, a purpose for singing that was dear to her soul. She understood song to be not the graceful ornament to a genteel life, but a sacred healing ... the sound, the pitches, the tones to flow across her listeners as healing rain. The beauty of this vision, though she could not have put it into words, was the central purpose of her life. Really the pain Laurele felt was not the pain of parting from the body, but the pain of seeing this vision cut off with so little expression.

Now we see another cobblestone street and we hear the wheels of a wagon, an iron-tired wagon this time, sometimes on cobblestones, sometimes on dirt, and sometimes on streets of brick. This wagon is making its way slowly through a burnt-out city. That city is Richmond, Virginia, in the spring of 1865. The city has been bombarded for forty days. The bombardment is ending now, as the Union Army marches in, and refugees flee, mostly to the West.

Once again Nora is a young woman, very young here, fourteen perhaps; in the name of LYNNETTE. Once again her birth was to a gentle family -- genteel might be the better word – and she as a child has just begun to glimpse her life as a woman and her destiny despite the long, long war. Now with the arrival of that army so long feared, with the long days of bombardment, and the city burnt black, down to rubble mostly, lit only by fires … she is straining at the very limits of sanity.

She does not know where her parents are. She does not know

where her sisters are. She is following a wagon driven by a slave. Heaped on the wagon there are trunks, a dining room table, silver services in boxes wrapped in blankets, hidden as well as they could be under the load. There are dresses and coats heaped over all.

Lynnette is buffeted by the sounds around her, the sounds of horses in panic, the wagon itself and other wagons, the shouts and calls and the grunts of drivers … the burning, burning, burning all around, and occasionally, the sound of one or another house collapsing … then comes a huge sound, the explosion of the armories being blown up so that their stores of ammunition will not be captured by the enemy.

It is too much for Lynnette. She runs from the wagon and seeks shelter in the dark, so that the open sky of flying sparks is not above her. She crawls deeply into a ruined structure. It's almost dawn, and she has been there several hours, when the structure collapses. Lynnette is suffocated there.

So Richmond and suffocation are linked to this day in Nora's mind, and any family that places an emphasis on manners … and what's the word here? ... and on *social pretense*, tends to reawaken memories of those two genteel lives extinguished by violence.

Now let us look closely at an Egyptian life, not capped by violence at all. We see the fertile green plain that stretches on both sides of the Nile. There are clusters of palms, and stands of reeds, and crops in rows.

We see carts again, pulled by bullocks, which are emblems of prosperity here. These bullocks were emblems of abundant crops in a society that was durable, balanced, and successful.

This life was spent at a time that was far earlier than those Egyptian lives of which we have an archaeological record. This life was spent at a time when what we think of as religion was far more personal, and far smaller in scale, than what we see in the remnant of Egyptian civilization. For later in Egypt the temples and the priests and the whole structure of images and processions and festivals was huge, impersonal, and cumbersome, and was actually the celebration of God-Kings and their great power.

But at the time that Nora lived in Egypt it was a growing, manageable, medium-sized society experiencing prosperity and giving happiness to almost every citizen. So don't see gloomy pyramids and great temples. Don't see grim priests with shaven heads. It was not like that.

This was a society where livelihood could be had without slave labor, where great armies were not raised and sent to distant places, where people mostly lived in what today we would call medium-sized suburbs. We see the name Meru, M-E-R-U, once again a female.

But this time living to a full and happy old age, which in that time was into the forties for most individuals. But Meru lived into her fifties, and was admired for her serenity, her calmness, and her ability to train mothers.

She had the ability to convey by example, not so much with words, the healing power that she shared so freely with babies at a time in civilization when most babies did not survive the first year of life.

It was a golden time for her. It was a time not marked by religion, but marked instead by a comfortable and joyful sense of being at one with the earth, with the sky, and with a universe that provided freely.

It is the time mentioned a few moments ago, downstairs, when Nora asked if she knew Edgar Cayce in his experience as the ancient Egyptian leader known as Raa-Taa. Let us see if they encountered each other.

Hmmm ... well, we see Meru as a girl of about twelve, walking in a grassy field, wearing a simple -- what's the word for this? -- not a tunic, not a shift, but something intermediate between the two, the same garment every other woman wore to do housework and fieldwork. She's barefoot. And she comes across a party of officials, and they're not fearsome, they're not grim, they have no guards. They are walking and talking about irrigation, quite literally inspecting the works. And yes, Raa-Taa is among them. And he smiles at Meru, cordially, naturally, nothing cosmic here.

In that moment she senses her happy life ahead, and she has full confidence that as she matures and goes out into public life, so to speak, society will welcome her and support her. That glance and that fleeting touch made an impression in memory that has never been forgotten.

So Nora has looked in vain for government leaders as wise and as approachable and as much like her as he was. He was a man of indeterminate age, a reasonably handsome man, lightly dressed in white linen, wearing only a headband as a badge of office, and carrying a staff. Everything about this encounter was natural and unforced. There was no threat here, no aura of power.

That marked for Meru the moment when she passed from childhood into an adult status, for this society had no status that might be called "adolescent." And for her it was not the onset of the menses that marked that entry into adulthood, but the blossoming of confidence in the world and the community around her; that it would be kind, observant of the needs of mothers and children, in harmony with these abundant fields. It was a very happy moment and she had a life both happy and serene.

So it is not what's in the text of *There is a River*, or *My Life as a Seer,* it is the memories which come back like a river, Meru's own river, who knew what it was to be fully accepting of herself, to be confident that her knowledge and training and her body too were all adequate to make a good life in a beneficent society. And that vision will never be far from Nora today.

Now in this time, through prayer, that vision can be projected outward, not on the world of television news and headlines and ghastly movies, but onto the world of green fields, healthy cattle, free-flowing and clean waters, and orderly commerce. And these things might well be the subjects of Nora's prayers, so that she once again radiates that serenity outward.

The music of Nora is the music of Meru. It is not, was not, was never meant to be, a product to be championed in the competitive, sometimes savage world of professional performance. It is, was always meant to be, transparent in its methods, seemingly simple although in truth complex in its inner design. And meant to heal directly. Quite literally to rearrange the cells and even the atoms in the listeners, just as Meru formerly did.

Nora, don't picture a crude and abrupt deity, who caused the tumor whose trauma ended your musical career. It was not so. That tumor came about because these ears were physiologically tuned, but they reported to a brain and a memory housed in the aura about the body, that knew far truer sounds and harmonies than those that Nora, to be honest, had to endure.

For her soul knew a music without pride, a music without competition, a music utterly divorced from commercial considerations.

It was also a music divorced from religious ceremony. It was a music married to and at one with healing and the fundamental forces that create life in a human body.

Now, can those sounds be created again on this earth at this time?

Honestly, both the instruments and the ears have changed, but the vision still lives. However Nora would make music, by whatever means, as a performer or as a composer, that inner vision would prevail over the technological limitations of modern-day music making, and touch her listeners in precisely the same way. That is not the vision of music performance that she was taught to have. But it is the vision of music performance that lives, and is healthy, and is still creative in her soul.

Now listen closely: the form, the style, the text: all are unimportant. The tones, the rhythms, the sonority of the harmonies, are all-important. Do you understand, Nora?

Nora: Yes, yes, yes.

Brian: We see that you do. So, don't seek a commercial audience. Seek innocent ears, and heal them.

It doesn't matter if you so label what you do. For the person that you are, and even the body that you have, are such that when you take your place before a group of children or adults they will be utterly for you. They will not judge you. They will not expect Nora to produce a polished, aggressive, marketable music. They will know immediately that what she has to give is her truest self. And they will listen in that spirit. Do you understand?

Nora: Yes, yes.

Brian: Now was it your purpose to come here and be a performer? No. It was your purpose to find again faith in life, not faith in God -- faith in life, the stream of life that forms a civilization, the stream of life that grows a crop and truly powers a river -- find faith in that. And live a long life, fed inwardly by the beauty of your own understanding, freely shared with those innocents who need to hear it. It's not about famous recordings, the name of your group, or fame. It's about that healing.

Yes, the hearing is gone in one ear. So you have one ear to listen to the music as you make it, and a spiritual ear to listen to the music of your past. In equal parts, do you understand?

Nora: Yes, yes, yes.

Brian: Yes, the sound waves and the timbre you produce on an instrument or with your voice will lack in some dimensions, but your mind will not. Mind is the builder, and mind is also the projector, the sonorous bell in the ethers that will convey what you have to give. Do you understand?

Nora: Yes.

Brian: We see that you do … that civil war has ended and this country, this land you live in, will not in your lifetime see that destruction again. Your guardians will never, never expose you to the risk of suffocation again, not figuratively and not literally. Do you understand?

Nora: Yes.

Brian: You are blessed with that protection. The violence of the mob, the fury of revolution, the excitement of political change; you have no part in these. You have no responsibility to watch closely or follow developments. You have no obligation to be brave in the face of that kind of riotous social change.

Your job is different at this time in life. Protect yourself. Don't watch the war news, don't watch the crime news, don't read the editorial page. Do you understand?

Nora: Yes.

Brian: They are not necessary to sustain you. They exact a toll. Don't pay it anymore. You do not care, you deeply do not care, about the outward trappings of high birth. They were really suffocating to you. Neither do you care about the stadium crowd at the rock and roll show, or the spectators at the parade as the eighty-piece marching band comes down the street.

No. You care about those innocent ears and those young souls, looking now, just as they looked in that ancient life of yours, for a note that reminds them of why they came and how they prepared. And you can give it. Sometimes you'll give it just holding a child, without a sound, because it's in you. Babies perceive these things, perfectly well. Do you understand?

Nora: Yes, yes.

Brian: Sometimes you hear … you hear these sounds, actually and truly being emitted by the wind chimes at the A.R.E. Always seemingly in another room --- you can't quite hear them distinctly. But you hear the truth of them in your soul. Trust that.

When you have made this serenity your own, with a year or two of practice, the ringing bell of your soul will draw to you a man utterly different from those you've been with before. Definitely a man who is a parent. Definitely a man who will look past clothing, appearance, accessories, and see Isis and Hathor shining through your being. Do you understand that? Isis was the Divine Mother.

Nora: Oh, yes, yes …

Brian: Hathor was the face of the Divine Mother, who exactly as the Virgin Mary did, directly sustained life for infants and young mothers. That is your connection to the Divine in this incarnation.

We don't have anymore the rituals that invoke the presence of Isis and Hathor. They've been lost for thousands of years. The visual evidence we have is not of their manifestation in the best times, but of their imagery in the decayed times, when the living truth of the beliefs had been lost. Consequently the surviving art of ancient Egypt has little appeal for you.

But if you will sit under the stars and look at the moon, the same moon that graces the head-dress of Hathor, where it is flanked on either side by the horns of a bullock, you'll feel it. It will give you not just peace but loving strength. And this meditation, this wordless, informal opening to the stars and moon, will quite literally pour the loving strength of Isis and Hathor into your soul.

You will recognize a gentle man who values fatherhood above all. And he will see in you a person who will recognize his value, and a love that can last. Pray for it. Hold it in mind when you're under the moon and the stars, and it will be drawn to you. You don't have to make it happen. And it will be a smile that gives him away, his smile. You'll hear the doors open.

Conductor: There are no more written questions. We would like to know if there is anything else that should or could be given at this time?

Brian: Yes. There are healings that are needed in this body. Virginia Beach can be a hospital city for you, Nora. The body workers, the gentle teachers of dance, the worship services you can experience in this building, at the A.R.E., and in other congregations – these are your hospital. As your mental body reassembles your deep understandings, your physical body will let go of the panic it has felt at times when others drew near, and so permit these healings to take hold.

So seek those body workers, seek those worship experiences. Recognize that nothing outward, no creed, no idea, no book, no cult, is necessary for you to heal and heal perfectly, and enter on a long new life.

Do that with your time in Virginia Beach. You won't be here the rest of your life. It's not important, there's time enough to do what you've come here to do, which is to heal the body. We won't go into the details, but you're tired and there is dis-coordination in places: within the stomach, in its coordination with the gall bladder, in the Ph of your blood particularly as it affects energy in the long muscles of your legs – all of these conditions can be corrected. That is a blessing and a promise, and with that we are through for now.

When the reading was completed Nora and I talked for half an hour. I said little, as I usually do in these sessions, and she said a lot. She cried some, also usual for these sessions, because so much of her innermost life had been laid out in language. That is a touching experience for us all. And it is a lovely one for me, because unlike my teacher, and unlike Edgar Cayce, I remember what I have seen, and it is an intimate and very human experience of connection. Not so objective, once it's over!

Nora took this advice to heart. Asthma and panic attacks faded from her experience, not overnight, but over months, as she recognized the patterns that underlay her reactions each day and she gradually changed them.

Conducted by Jill Allbrandt
Given at the Fellowship of the Inner Light
Virginia Beach, May, 2011
Nora was present

Aleisha

Chapter 3

ALEISHA WAS A YOGA TEACHER who knew that she was part of a soul family, but the idea of a Teacher in a Mystery School of Life was unknown to her. She did believe that her life and her choices were guided and shaped according to some purpose, and she believed that teaching yoga was part of that purpose.

All I knew of her was that her older sister had died only a year before in a climbing accident in the American West. When Aleisha appeared in my sunroom for a reading, dressed like a graduate student in gray sweats, I met a woman of thirty-two, dark-haired and slender, pretty, with flashes of humor that appeared despite her aura of sadness.

She was coping with her difficulties but she was really vulnerable; that was my first impression.

Despite this she seemed youthful and fundamentally good-humored, in some ways like a recent college graduate, still testing life for its possibilities, not seriously engaged on a career or a path.

As we talked for a few moments before our reading, she described her seven years of yoga training and how she had tried to use those tools to lift herself up. She said she was a meditator and had been since her teen years. And she had shared many outdoor adventures with her sister Margaret, which made Margaret's fall from a rocky spire much too immediate for Aleisha, because she could picture it, and truly relive it so clearly, even though she had been far away when it happened.

Then she also revealed that only a few months before the reading she had been trekking in Latin America with her boyfriend Jack, a combat veteran of American wars in the Middle East, when in an outburst fueled by drugs he had beaten her so savagely that bones in her face were broken.

At the point she came for her reading the shock of this unexpected trauma was still fresh for Aleisha, and I could feel it too. How had a life so normal turned into this?

She was sad, of course, but she labeled that as depression. Additionally her periods had ceased entirely at only thirty-one after several years of irregularity. Finally she said that she had tried to use the understandings learned in teaching yoga to cope with these losses but she would not hide that she was suffering.

> Mica, the Conductor here, asked Aleisha's first question: "I'd like to proceed more truly in my life purpose. What can I know about it that will help, and what has or may hinder me?"

The Record Keeper this time was a dark, curly-haired woman who appeared to be about fifty. Aleisha's Teacher in Spirit? I thought so. She handed the book to me and to my surprise stood beside me so that we read it together. She held my upper arm as we read, as we might with someone in mourning, and I could feel that kind of support radiating from her to me. In that moment I needed it, for I was feeling Aleisha's losses too. The transcript of the reading begins here:

> We have this book. It's handed to us by a woman, in appearance … perhaps fifty. Flowing brown hair, clear, clear blue eyes; and she holds the book to her chest for a moment and then hands it to me. We open it together. It's an unusual book. It is bound in polished green leather. It's tall, probably when we're on earth 15 inches tall, as much as 12 inches wide, and thick. It's bound as rare editions were bound in the 19th and early 20th century, and as we open it we see not just words or entries but type, type set as if in letterpress. And from these words arise colors, a swirl of colors that fill this room. And some we've seen on earth and some we have not.

Taken together we see a life prepared for with study before you came here, Aleisha. Study of what we might call the classics of western literature, thought and philosophy. And these things are safe in your soul, in your deepest being. You've absorbed their values and while you came with other purposes as well, you did come to live a life informed by these classic values. Let's go to the questions.

At first we see a towering mountain with a trail meant for cross-country skiing. Then we see books in leather bindings as we might find them in the study of a lifelong scholar. Taken together, these symbols speak of a life path literally meant to draw its values from what is written or programmed in that wilderness earth in the American West.

These values are not written in modern language at all. They vibrate with the understandings that were formed after the cataclysms that really produced Atlantis and major changes in world civilization, the vast majority of which are utterly lost to what history we have.

What are those values? Strength is one value, and generosity so broad in its scope that modern Americans can hardly comprehend people who come to treat, not their nations, but their *societies* as family, with cooperation as the greatest value. Peaceful cooperation, intelligent cooperation, and cooperation as equals, without the desire to take advantage, or gain hegemony over indigenous peoples, or less fortunate peoples, or immigrant peoples, or survivors from whatever catastrophes and wars have plagued the earth across the span of your lifetime, Aleisha.

This has been prepared not just for you but for many. Prepared to have these memories return and shape a generation, not just in America, but all over the earth. On each continent, there are places and heights prepared to draw these memories to the surface for you and for many others too. So yours will more and more be a far-traveled life.

As a person your values have been thoroughly shaped in classic American and Western and European molds. This was done before you came here. Those ideas will be put to the service of purposes far greater in scope, purposes that have not really been seen in civilizations on this earth in ten to twelve thousand years.

From that mountaintop view the reading turned toward the losses Aleisha had suffered. Turned not abruptly, but gently and personally.

Goodness! That was given on a high and an abstract plane. There's a saying among therapists that depression is what we feel as roots reach for water … in our beings, Aleisha, in our beings. Your roots are deep inside. What waters them? The events of your life. The people you love. The places you love. The experiences that you undergo, some of which you have not recognized as being important to you because they didn't have your name on them.

You, like others in your generation, are a quite sensitive barometer to what we're going to call world events.

We're not going to call them geopolitical realities. We're not going to call them trends or changes. We're not even going to call them religious beliefs. These are great forces that are moving the populations of the earth toward a new future. Barely, barely glimpsed, but you in common with others in your generation are experiencing them as forces which leave you feeling ungrounded.

Where can you put your feet? How can you walk forward?

All of this is so different from what most Americans think, at least in your parents' generation, that you will be wondering for some years to come, "How am I supposed to make a living? How is this a career?" But you will be taken care of, Aleisha. Opportunities will come.

You did not come to walk a conventional path of employment and career. You came to prepare a future which will burst upon the world unannounced and unrecognized.

This future is already begun but it is not recognized anywhere. It is not named, it is barely apparent even in the art, the music, and the poetry of this time. And that is why you must learn it on the high grounds amid the great rocks and snows of the Western heights. These things will come to mind not as words or principles or facts, but as wordless changes in your own motives. Gradually you will learn to follow those changing motives.

Then the reading turned again and focused on Aleisha's identity as a teacher of yoga. But the dimensions called up here were little explained in her yoga training.

Aleisha, that's what you elected to experience. Your earth and your path are inside you. You will be quite mature in age before you're able to give words to what guides you or what principles you are living, but already you are able to apprehend and follow them as quiet voices, even though those voices at this time create confusion, doubt, and a feeling that everything should be clearer.

You have the questions you brought here today: why are you not proceeding, as your classmates and your contemporaries are proceeding, to lives that are a little more concrete and a little more comprehensible?

You did elect to take this on in order to be truly a participant and servant to that which is new. It is proceeding out of all of the earth and will always be apprehended by you through your senses within.

You are not a prophet so much as you are a pioneer. What you will do will be your contribution, not so much what you say or write. Your job will be to touch others, and they will follow you on a path to wholeness.

We don't mean to diminish your losses at all. These were, they are, major events. They have opened to you a look into the meaning of human existence comparable to what we feel when we stand on the rim of the Grand Canyon and look down. These things do come to people in their twenties and their thirties. It takes years to wrap words and concepts around them, and it will take you years as well, but they've already changed you.

For Jack, the experiences that have closed so many doors to him are in fact a human tragedy. They're not new. What war does to us has been much the same in every culture and in every time.

Then the direction of the reading turned once more to Aleisha's most personal needs and gifts as the conductor asked Aleisha's second question: "My sister's passing, the violence that came to me through Jack. What impressions have these made on my soul? What do I need to know about these? My periods have stopped. What is going on here?" The answer began,

You will not be able to proceed through life with people whose trust and faith in life itself has been suppressed and dissolved away by violence, the events of war, even the events of political dislocation and the refugee life. You will love and trust those who draw on inner strength and on spiritual values. These will be your close companions in the life ahead.

You loved your sister. You also understood her as a human being. Her life had its shadows, and you felt them keenly, but as things go in this century, they were in the normal range. You will see her again. She will return to your life stream.

Not soon. Her own recovery will be measured in earth years, for the end of this life came to her unexpectedly. She is reassembling her body of light where she is. That's a slow process in earth time. It is a tender and a gentle and a beautiful process and one you might do well to study, through learning of near-death and end of life experiences. The clues to the road map are there.

You loved her. She loved you. That's the important part of what you experienced together. Has your life been diminished by her passing? Yes, in the short run it has. That will be corrected as the years go by. Do you understand?

Aleisha: Yes. I think I do.

Brian: All right. You do see life differently because of these two events. You don't have words, this channel doesn't have words, for the changes that have been wrought inside your being.

Now we're going to look at your endocrine system, at the reasons why your period, your reproductive cycles, the body structures of reproduction in your own body have not functioned in an ordinary way…

This is going to be hard for this channel to express. You have not yet made a choice at the soul level whether to bear children in this life. When you make that choice, the requisite adjustments will be made in your body and in your endocrine system. Your body is not now, nor has it been, ideal for conception. Nor will it be, nor has it been, ideal to carry and bear safely an infant. Do you understand what I am saying?

Aleisha: Yes.

Brian: This door has been held shut for you by means that have not been comfortable but were necessary for your soul. The best thing you can do about this is to examine the question of being a mother, not the concept of motherhood, but *being* a mother, with all your being, and all your prayers, and all your meditative tools, and make a decision that rings right to the ground level of your soul. And when you've made that decision, that which has been written in your body will be altered to suit your choice. Do you understand?

Aleisha: Yes.

Brian: We are not saying you cannot bear children. We are not saying you cannot become pregnant. We are saying it will be a unique, I don't want to say 'troublesome,' but a unique walk which will have to be undertaken consciously and with care. It is possible. But you have not, until this point in your life, been aware that this choice is in front of you in these terms. Do you understand what was just said?

Aleisha: Yes.

Brian: The conditions of it in your body will right themselves when you have made this decision. You do not need to undertake … I'm going to call them "desperate medical measures.'"

The whole area of fertility and reproduction and even endocrinology, frankly, remains a dark hole to modern medicine. Don't put yourself in those hands. Trust your yoga, your meditative understandings, and the wisdom of your body. That wisdom is unique just as your body is unique. It proceeds out from your life purpose. What is average, what is said to be normal, is less relevant to you than it is to most people, and it's not so relevant even to most people. Do you understand?

Aleisha: Yes.

Brian: Your body and your health proceed forth from your inmost being directly and in full and joyful cooperation with that which guides you through this life. We're calling that the Source of your Being.

Is that a grandfather in a blue robe perched on a cloud directing the mortals below? It is not. What it really is defies words, defies religion, defies conceptual thinking.

It is unbelievably diverse. You can know it by walking with it. Its hand will never be hidden from you. Love flows from that Source into your being and into your life, but not according to any religious or cultural or historic formula. You can only know it by seeking not just its will, although that too; but its *direction*. Do you understand that?

Aleisha: Yes.

Brian: Listen closely to your life. Listen closely to what and whom you love. And you will not lose your way nor will you lose your health. You have provided this body and this life plan, honestly Aleisha, with radiant health. And the more truly you walk the path that you have designed, the more clearly it will manifest.

In this reading we have met for the first time three things that are fundamental to every reading. The first is the "Teacher in Spirit." When first we begin to meditate and pray, expecting to enter into a live relationship with the Creator, literally by the light we emit we attract to ourselves one or more teachers who come to guide us in our growth.

Usually they remain invisible to the seeker and the gifts they bring are subtle, as little remarked as the influence of the vibrations of the mountain earth pictured here. But they are perfectly crafted to help the seeker grow in the light of the Record. As these teachers regard our lives and our souls they see ahead and they see behind, into former lives, into our futures, into our sojourns between lives, and into our larger communities too -- more than we can compass. This relationship is private. But when we become helpers or channels we share in those gifts. Through our intuition in the helping situation these energies are opened to us, not by doctrine or concepts.

In this reading we also meet "the body of light." That is the aura, of course, and it survives death. It also carries the wavelengths and the colors and lights which will unfold into our beings as our lives go on. There is a great deal more to it than we generally credit at this point in the twenty-first century. It holds the keys to healing, to integrity, to our identity too. There will be more about this body of light in Chapter 10, the story of Chris.

Finally we also encounter the Source of Aleisha's Being. This entity has many names in many traditions. I see it at work in these reading situations, I sense its presence, but I can't really produce language that is adequate to what is really there. My command of traditional Christian concepts won't do, so I'll leave that comparison to others better educated than I am. But as you read these soul stories pay attention to how it appears and how it shapes these lives.

At that point in the reading experience we asked as we always do toward the end, "Is there anything else that could or should be given at this time?"

> Brian: Forgiveness is required of all of us in connection to the people we've loved and been close to. It will require your paying attention to bad feelings you have, which may surface. Honestly, in your being some of those will have their roots in former life experiences with those individuals. Such is the nature of your sensitivities that you feel them. Do you understand?

Aleisha: Yes.

Brian: Do not be shocked or surprised. Every dream has a meaning. That meaning is not clothed in obscurity. As you wake from a dream with feelings flowing, enter prayer on the spot for those figures you have seen. Dreams are not riddles or word puzzles. They are pictures of *forces* at work in your being and forces entering your being from spirit. We all have to learn to pray for ordinary human beings, even if they're drunks or violent or thieves or mentally ill. Do you understand?

Aleisha: Yes.

Brian: They too have lives to make and paths to walk. We do not have to fall into the error of, "if I pray this loving prayer for this person, then I have to help this person work it out." You do not. Leave that to God and the Angels. Do you understand?

Aleisha: Yes.

Brian: And honestly your karma will fall away as you do. Do you understand that?

Aleisha: Yes.

Brian: We do have links with the souls we're attracted to. We have links with the souls we despise as well. Both need to be dissolved in the light and both need it equally. Do you understand that?

Aleisha: Yes.

Brian: It is not easy to pray for those who do you harm. It is not easy to pray for those who choose to stand for that which you know very well is destructive, hopeless, or evil. We are equipped to do it, however. It's part of human purpose to do that. What in our time we get wrong is the notion that we are then bound to them. No. We do it on purpose to release those karmic bonds even though we may have experienced them as all good. Do you understand?

Aleisha: Yes.

Brian: You're praying for the freedom of those souls with whom you have intersected. You need to be doing that. Not with conventional judgements, not with conventional language. All of us in our time will love people who are destructive or mentally ill or seriously handicapped or on the bottom of the social order. And all of us will love those who in our experience shine as beacons of love and light and health, and when we pray for them our energy blends with theirs and they give those gifts to us. Do you understand?

Aleisha: Yes.

Brian: All right. So you need to be making those prayers. It's part of your yogic life, a part that the yoga that's taught in America tends to leave out.

What followed in this reading was dietary advice because she asked for it. The suggestions were unique to Aleisha, things that had worked well for her in former lives. This is often the case, because our souls and our bodies both remember. Then the reading turned again to the immediate.

Brian: In the year to come, you will knit about your heart, literally knit, new understandings. Courage will return to your being and the joy of the heart will return to your being too. Until you sense that heart as the fountain of joyful strength and energy that it was designed to be, get adequate rest, schedule recreation in the outdoors, and don't enter into a romantic relationship.

Your heart has been injured. Give it a year to recover. It wasn't part of your plan, but such blows happen to most of us. Honor those blows and those injuries and take a year to recover. That's important for you. We're not saying that heart symptoms or heart problems are in your future, not soon and not later, either, only that you have sustained a loss that is telling on your heart. Let's mend it.

Aleisha's teacher in spirit was real to me, because I felt her hand on my arm and looked into her eyes. Aleisha felt her presence too but had no language for what she felt. But she left the reading experience buoyed up, with feelings flowing, and with a sense that what she had heard was true even though there was much she had never heard before.

How then could she hold on to something so elusive, so like a dream, so little buttressed by earthly advice? Somehow she did. She was touched and she knew it, and she went forward believing that she was not alone. That is part of the reading experience for most seekers – the explanations matter less than the experience of being touched by something that arises directly out of her own being.

Given in Bradenton, Florida
Conducted by Mica Glasberg
May, 2018.

Maggie and Sophia, a Master Physician

Chapter 4

MAGGIE WAS QUITE ILL WHEN WE DID THIS READING. It was a distant reading, done while she was in New York and I was at home in Florida. Maggie chose not to be on the phone because she was too distressed to remain calm or receptive, either one, and she knew that. She had literally argued with me during previous readings and we didn't want to experience that again.

A doctor she had seen was insisting that her gallbladder needed to be removed immediately. She was helpless with abdominal pain, actually unable to walk. Her distress and her pain were genuine.

That had been a question at times, for Maggie had been a drama major in college, and at times the expressions of her inner life were a little overwhelming to those close to her. In her fifties Maggie was a singer and performer who lived a gypsy life from a minivan, even though she had a New York apartment. On this day her minivan was disabled by a fallen tree and she was stranded in the City.

As a folk singer Maggie's voice was full of joy and good humor and she was widely recognized for that. But the creative part of her being sometimes seemed to turn against her when symptoms appeared, and she focused on them, and then those symptoms multiplied and seemingly shifted shape.

Self-love: easy words to use, but not always so easy to manifest, especially when, as in Maggie's life, early and prolonged experiences of emotional abuse had left her riddled with doubts and bad feelings that came up in her times alone.

Her mother was a Broadway actor with a big blind spot for abusive and alcoholic men. Maggie herself had remained single and throughout her life had spent a great deal of time in spiritual communities.

She brought her music and her own considerable esoteric knowledge to those communities in several states, and she had good friends of long standing in them too. So I knew that she would be familiar with whatever esoteric concepts we might reference.

But this reading was instructive to me for another reason. Here I had a Master Physician from ancient Greece sharing the reading experience from spirit, applying her healing energy to Maggie, and instructing me how to scan a body thoroughly and more effectively than I had been doing — and more lovingly too.

Paul's teaching was founded on this, that we all can do such things, including miracles. The experience of the Terraces and the Temple were fundamental to learning how to turn on our subtle senses. These are the senses we employ when we operate in the spiritual body, something we all can learn to do.

In Chapter 7 I will explain the Meadow, the Terraces, and The Temple as they were employed here. These comprise the preparation for meditation that I actually use before every reading. They are read aloud to me by the conductor while I follow into that guided meditation, which is what my readings actually are. I learned them when I took Paul's basic Experience -- not a "course" -- in 1977, and I have used them daily ever since, mostly in private, for I don't do readings every day.

Working with Paul, this simple imagery with its accompanying emotions became a journey through an ever-changing spiritual landscape, an infinitely variable experience rich with information and connection.

What follows is the transcription of a sound recording made on a voice recorder in a single one-hour session, just as I did with Nora. This method is standard for me and this is one of 400-plus readings I have done in this same way for many kinds of seekers over the last ten years. Most of my readings, perhaps eighty percent, deal as directly with health and the body as this one does.

You will see here that simply revealing what is wrong, or what is at work deep in consciousness, is rarely enough to effect a healing. Changes, changes in action and in attitudes, are almost always required of the seeker. Truly the beauty of what is revealed can help the seeker make the changes, as can the experience of connection to one's innermost being, but the changes must be made.

Here, transcribed from this session's recording, my daughter Susana leads me into the preparation for meditation that precedes every reading I do. She conducted throughout:

> Conductor: Let us enter a meadow now, seeking peace and the knowledge that all of earth's beauty, its life, and the God that sustains these, will create in us in this hour the peace to hear, comprehend, and act anew.
>
> See tall grass waving in the sunlight that bathes this meadow. See the mighty tree with the lightning scar in its center. Feel the earth, warm and moist beneath your feet, and smell its goodness. Sense the sunlit space of the air around you. Hear a brook tumbling over stones at the edge of the meadow.
>
> Hear leaves rustling and birds singing. See squirrels in the branches, and rabbits around the roots of oaks, maples, and cedars. See those roots reaching deep into earth. Invest these plants and earthly things with love, just as they invest love in you.
>
> Leave the meadow behind you now and start up a mountain path. We are going to the summit of this mountain to a sacred, protected, and dedicated space to seek understanding for Maggie in the light of her Akashic Record.
>
> Come to the first terraced garden, all in red. Bottlebrush, carnations, and tulips here are all bursting with life. Touch them, breathe in their energy. Feel your limbs and abdomen lifted, made young, flushed with circulating blood. Feel expectancy arrive and build. In this red garden we feel the quickening that precedes the spirit. Now leave the red garden behind.

Walk higher up the path. Come to an orange garden, scattered with autumn leaves. The earth is moist and warm here. Smell wood smoke. Hear leaves crackle beneath your feet. They sail around you and land with faint plops on the surface of a pond. Here you leave behind old ideas that are worn out. Here lay down all earthly concerns and worries. Slip them off like worn-out clothes dropped to earth. Then go higher.

Come to a yellow garden. Daffodils, tulips, and crocuses greet us here as we walk to a spring. Read the signs of Easter all around, new life, new beginnings, new understandings. Smell lemon blossoms. Hear a choir in a church just out of sight, singing "Welcome happy morning, age to age shall say." See the faces of your brothers and sisters who sing in these choirs and pause for a moment to love them. Climb on.

Enter a green terraced garden. Taste pines in the air. Sense the arrival of your own Teacher. He will guide us to the Record; be a gatekeeper; and protect this body and keep it safe while the spirit goes on its higher journey.

Now go higher. Enter a blue garden. Hear waves lapping on the shore of a clear blue mountain lake. Light reflects off a sandy bottom. We are surrounded by blue-bonnets and wildflowers in bunches. Here serenity blooms, filling the throat with a glow of energy that aids the speaking of truth.

Go higher then, and enter a violet terrace alive with orchids. Feel the presence of your own Source expand, bring you vision, and fill your being. Breathe in the power and the grace of this experience.

Pass through the layer of cloud that hid the summit from view. Walk into sunlight. Now cross the space there and see all above you the vast sky of space. Soak up the sunlight, breathe air that is fresh and electrically charged, walk through a mountain meadow spotted with lacy wildflowers and white blossoms.

See your Temple just ahead and draw near to it. Between you and the Temple there is a still reflecting pool. Enter the pool and feel all that is heavy washed away. Feel the soul emerge, cleansed and ready for the Temple, clothed in a simple white tunic; no emblems, no robes.

Climb one dozen shallow steps and enter. Pass through the outer columns and enter the inner chamber. See light shining on marble walls; blossoms on hanging plants; pools set in the wide floors. Settle before an altar. This altar is lit by the one light that lights every man and every woman who enters the earth. Here we are the sons and daughters of God, one with the light and with all sensate creatures.

Brian: What has been overlooked or inadequately seen? We have looked in the last year at the anger at siblings and others, at the past-life patterns, at the lessons of Maggie's soul too. Help us to see anew into this body and this physiology at this time.

The conductor speaks again: Maggie is in New York. She was born on the date September —-th, 1961, in New York, New York and christened with the name Margaret ———-.

(The transcript of the body of the reading begins here:)

Brian: Now I see a golden book and a hand poised, not to read but to write in this book. The book is slender and small. The gold is worked in a lacy pattern. This is the notebook of a master physician, truly a Sophia from ancient Greece, one who understands not only the body and healing, but the nature of woman in manifestation: what is unique in women's bodies, in their lives, and in the tasks they undertake.

She opens this book, and then with her hands she shines a light on Maggie's body. She starts at the head and moves her hands just a few inches away from the body, from the crown and past the ears, past the eyes, the nose, and the mouth, healing and diagnosing at the same time.

She passes her hands over the shoulders, down the arms and elbows and into the hands. She relaxes Maggie's hands and puts them face up in the anatomical position. She puts her hands over Maggie's chest, checks and regulates the heart, its rhythms, and its electrical fields. She passes her hands down the trunk, paying special attention to the lungs, the great blood vessels, the spleen, the liver; and down the abdomen, looking closely at the gallbladder, and looking at its interaction with the stomach and with the endocrine system.

She looks at the stomach, its fluids, its membranes, and the walls of the stomach too, both the lining and the outer walls. She looks at the stomach's links to other organs in the body. She looks at the valves above and below that admit food from the esophagus and transmit stomach contents to the small intestine.

While she's in the upper trunk, she looks at the adrenals and at the various glands that regulate and furnish both energy and fluids to the small intestine. She looks at the large intestine and the rectum, at the kidneys and the bladder, and at the urethra; and then at the reproductive organs, including the womb and the vagina.

She looks at the walls of the abdominal sac inside and out. She looks for any sign of fomenting infection, and at the liquid-filled membranes that contain and support these organs; and she looks within the organs themselves.

She looks for what is fresh and what is old. She literally wraps her hands around these organs to listen to them, to assess their present state. She pours healing energy into them, now green; now gold; now pink. She moves to the hips and the spine, particularly thoracic, lumbar and sacral spine, looking at alignment, nerve signals, the state of the cerebrospinal fluid, the cord itself, looking for scars, injuries, signs of infection.

She looks at the ball and socket joints, the pelvis in general, the long bones in the leg, and the blood manufactories in those bones. She looks at the knees, the bones, the lower leg, the bones of the feet.

When a channel first learns to do readings, she or he practices – always in a group setting – imagining these organs and their symptoms. Even though the images she uses may be as simple as a child's book on the human body, the more she lets language flow she will experience "hits" frequently, according to her degree of empathy and the harmony in the group with whom she practices.

This has been borne out in hundreds of group trainings in my experience. Only in time does the information become detailed and error-free. And remedies, when they appear, are usually systemic and simple. They are also unique to each soul and to each body, not meant to be applied in a general way to others. This is not Western medicine, but soul medicine, and every soul has different memories and different Records.

To embrace these methods and exclude the input of experienced physicians would be foolish in the extreme. Instead it becomes the responsibility of the practitioner to form and maintain relationships with capable and sympathetic physicians, nurses, and therapists, and with them build a support network. Over time it remains the job of the channel or the healer to be thorough, open-minded, and detail-oriented.

I believe these principles hold true for intuitive healers of every kind. Likewise it is the responsibility of the seeker to check the accuracy of results with capable health professionals.

Brian: And what has Sophia found? Inflammation in many places, inflammation sufficient to cause these organs to complain when they're asked to do the ordinary jobs these organs do.

She has looked very closely at this gallbladder. She says, "Yes, it's in distress. At this point, it cannot handle the gall that gallbladders store and employ." She says, 'The problem is not structural.' She sees "inflammation here, but no sign of infection." She says plainly: "It would be pointless to remove this gallbladder."

She points then to the exit valve of the stomach, inflamed and at times, even in the last few days, bleeding. It has contracted so hard that it's injured its own soft tissues trying to keep stomach contents from entering that small intestine. These stomach contents have been so badly out of chemical balance that they would quite literally burn the inner surfaces, of the small intestine. What makes them so?

Ulcerations in the interior wall of the stomach, not through and through ulcers, although they do bleed from time to time. They are the cause of the burning pain. Are these ulcers from stress? Are they from infection? Are they from deficiency in the blood or the physiologic fluid supply? Let us ask those questions.

I'm going to have to unfold some of these symbols … this stomach has quite forgotten how to look forward to a meal. Forgotten how to create, as stomachs do, an appropriate balance in digestive fluids, meal-by-meal, mixing them with what's taken in; plus handling the highly acidic fluids that are generated by anger and panic alternating in this body's emotional state. These ulcers are quite small, but painful, and we see more than two dozen. They are in a state of "General Quarters." They are in battle … against what enemy? They do not know.

We'll come back to a remedy for this. Those remedies which physicians employ for ulcers would be appropriate for these ulcers. Of course, to ingest these remedies in an upset state, or even with food of any kind, will compound the problems. If it's elected to take these medications, take them with a fast, at least three days, and pay close attention to how the mind is occupied in the course of this fast.

For this body, for this person, to be immersed in music is the way to occupy this mind. Not walking outdoors, not in this February season. Not on the telephone. But immersed in music only, and in gentle light, as, for example, candlelight.

But these recommendations are not primary here. These recommendations are secondary. More importantly, what can be done to reverse this pattern in this stomach and permit it, once again, to secrete and process appropriate digestive juices?

As Maggie has heard from these Records once before, compassionate, present, hands-on nursing care is the best solution for this stomach. She needs feminine love. She needs feminine, merciful hands. Her body will know what to do with that energy.

This is not a time to go it alone. This is not a time to be behind the wheel, navigating in the dark through snow, rain, or sleet … not wholly an accident that your vehicle has been disabled, Maggie. You need to seek nursing care and stay put. On this, our physician is crystal clear … and expert, expert nursing care. Well-meaning friends, even alternative healers, should yield to skilled, professional and compassionate nurses, and that's a strong recommendation here.

Now let's look at the situation in that small intestine and all those attendant organs that help it do its multi-sided job. This small intestine is literally pitted from acid contents. The small intestine is ... knotted is not the word, but parts of it have constricted … trying to protect those sensitive inner surfaces from the damage of further exposure to acid fluids. That's painful. This intestine needs a rest.

It needs a rest from the ingestion of solid foods. It needs a rest from the pressure and anxiety of Maggie attempting to take care of herself. This situation has spiraled beyond the range of what Maggie can take care of herself. She needs to rest under care. Honestly, the nurses are more important than the physicians on this case. They need to be professionals. They need to have knowledge. They need to comfort and give succor, and they need to be free from ... please, to help you, they need to be free from the practiced recital of the histories. They need to be free to care for this body. A water fast too, and bed rest of course.

Now let's look at this large intestine. It's in better shape than the small intestine. I'm seeing a lot of gas, a lot of distention, which makes pain. Likewise, it needs a rest. It was never designed to complete the job the small intestine is designed to do. The bowel is made to extract water from alkaline organic material. It's been a long time since this bowel has seen alkaline organic material. Nurses understand this. They understand what a fast is. They understand what a bland diet is, and this body needs both of those things, and bed rest.

This woman physician says, "We have in these days medications to calm your mind, to lift your anxiety, to take the edge off your anger, which you have entertained so long. This is anger at the injustices that have been visited on you in your life. Accept those medications. The anxiety medications, the ulcer medications, the tranquilizing medications, you have need for all three. Trust the women who care for you."

Trust this Sophia, Maggie. She knows what you've been through. She's known you through many lives. She says, ever so serenely, "You are past the time for confrontations, past the time for reckonings, past the time for searching. You have come to the time for complete rest."

If you cut that rest short, Maggie, you can expect to go on as you have been. You have symptoms in almost every organ and structure in your body. You have a cascading parade of symptoms.

First one part of your body and then another part tries to compensate to make its neighbors right. Let it go, Maggie. It's time for a rest, complete bed rest in gentle, knowing, expert hands. When you feel that urge to talk -- to go over once again the histories! -- take a glassful of water into your mouth, and hold it for as long as you can. Cool that tongue. Be still. Your tongue is not your friend in this situation.

Accept the serenity of caregivers. Allow it into your being. Let it quite simply displace and defuse the questions, the conflicts and the pains. Your body is worn out by fighting, and truly, Maggie. This is the physician talking: "You've been fighting invisible enemies who live only in your own perceptions. Now it's time for a rest. Don't judge yourself. Don't judge anyone else either, but accept the help that will be offered. Accept the bed rest. Accept the nursing care. Truly, this body does know how to heal itself."

To answer the basic question, 'Are there undiscovered disease conditions in this body?' There are pockets of infection. There are pockets of yeast. There are microbes stored in the liver and various other places and even in the fluids in the body, in the abdominal cavity.

None are sufficient to overwhelm this body's innate healing energy.

Let your mental defenses down. You are not alone. Seek the help and the comfort of living women in the flesh, Maggie. Let your spiritual body rest.

Can you be healed from these conditions? You certainly can. The infections you have and the breakdowns in some organs — these things are transient. They can and they will be healed by the measures already in place, if you will rest.

Do you need the intervention of an expert physician on Earth? Not really, Maggie. You need the loving support of expert nurses instead. There's no judgment here. There are only things to be healed.

What we've listed for you are lesions; they are not fulminating disease or infectious conditions. This body can heal them with rest. The medications you've been given have been wisely chosen. The decision to forgo surgery on that gallbladder was a wise decision and, yes, guided from these planes. Don't seek and seek and seek until you find an unwise physician who will do that which will only compound your troubles. We hope you understand.

Let us look. Is there a missing element in these medications?

No. We're told to avoid Sulfa drugs or any drug which contains Sulfa, and many do. Even those drugs labeled as antibiotics often contain a dash of Sulfa, not good for this body at this time. Avoid the Aspirin compounds too. You have enough inflammation.

Avoid the soy and skim milk compounds that are used for liquid nourishment; they're difficult for any body, and they would compound the inflammations in this body at this time. Water is needed, and only water for at least three days. Those things which you crave as you come to the end of this three-day water fast will be the things you need. Just ask for them.

Now what more needs to be said about this body? *Crying out for rest!*

These symptoms in these last several weeks have been your body crying out for rest, rest from the driving, rest from the incessant hammering of an inquiring mind that says, "What is wrong with me?" At this point, Maggie, quite a few small things are wrong with you, but none of your major organs are in great difficulty. You don't have undetected infections seeking to break forth and occupy some organ. You have some of the ordinary infections most of us have most of the time. They will be, as they often are, suppressed by the antibiotics you're being given. Will they wipe those infections out? No, Maggie. A body that has no infections would be a most unusual body.

Do you have microbes, bacteria, organisms causing these problems? No. They play a role when trouble comes. Your body, like every body, is -- let's not call it a battleground -- let's call it a playground of microbes and bacterial organisms. Some are your friends; some are your enemies; and some switch sides as conditions change.

You are not in a fight for your life against an undiscovered enemy. What you are is exhausted. We hope you understand. Stay put, Maggie. Twenty-one days minimum.

Now we ask as we always ask, is there anything else that could or should be given at this time?

Yes. This first, Maggie. Your mother is very much with you at this time, very much a healer and a friend to you. Wiser, more present, indescribably more gentle than she knew how to be when she occupied the body and the personality in which you knew her.

She understands your situation. She understands your lessons too, but she's not here to teach you anything. She's watching over you. She's praying for you, steadily, and not desperately. She puts her finger to your lips and says, "Shh…peace, Maggie dear. Rest and listen."

Good advice, Maggie. There are others behind her, others who support her, others who pray for you; quite a few of them. They don't want to draw attention to themselves. They want you to rest and be at peace. When you've begun to settle into rest, Maggie, they will be there with you, making little jokes, putting little jokes on your tongue too, restoring your good humor, which is in fact your natural state and, honestly, Maggie, the number-one gift you asked for in this life; and it was given. That's what they'll do. That's a blessing and a promise, and, Maggie, with that, we will be through for now.

Did Maggie take this advice? No, not at first. She could not fathom putting herself in the hands of living nurses in a real medical setting. Nurses in spirit she could have accepted! She delayed, and when in a few months she was ready to accept hospitalization, there was no doctor in the picture to make it happen.

I know Maggie to be a loving and informed woman, full of good humor and bubbling over with song in her ordinary state. I know too that she could be seen as a hypochondriac, a label that once accepted would do her little good.

Yet at this point in her life old injuries had reawakened and come to dominate her consciousness, thanks to conflict with siblings over an inheritance. Those conflicts had in fact come to court actions. The stress had been too much for Maggie and her body was genuinely in distress. Her difficulties at the time of the reading were painful and disabling, but not quite life-threatening, at least not yet.

Maggie believed strongly that she was a victim. Over and over she rehearsed the wrongs done to her. Whether those were real or only subjective, the climate that victim consciousness created in her body – built with all the creative energy she could command -- was the fundamental note of her illnesses.

In time, about a year, she did find a wise physician on earth and she did accept the hospitalization that was recommended. She suffered acute symptoms through that year, as she had done at other times in the past. She carried on in her minivan and visited many emergency rooms as she traveled, taking her rest in two-and three-day increments until she finally found the courage to accept the extended stay that she really needed. Did this reading experience help her? I can't be sure. Has she made the biggest step of all, to deliberately use her creativity, without or without the help of pharmaceuticals, to assert her own health? I don't know.

Given in Florida
Maggie was in New York City
Conducted by Susana Berry
February, 2018

Janet, Who Didn't Have to Come Back

Chapter 5

EVERY READING HAS SURPRISES TO GIVE. But some are so surprising in content and approach that if applied, they would turn the seeker's life on its head. What came for Janet and Sandra was just such a surprise. Sandra was the real seeker here, and she almost certainly wanted measures that would undo the losses suffered in recent months by her daughter Janet, 32, who has lived all her life with Down's Syndrome.

Sandra could not come for the reading. A single mom and a registered nurse, she was at work, while Janet was cared for at an adult day care center where she had been enrolled for years. Sandra had long depended on the center in order to work, but when Janet's doctor made a diagnosis of "obsessive compulsive disorder," the center decided they could no longer serve Janet. Sandra found that diagnosis difficult to accept. These developments inspired the reading request

Janet's grandmother came to the reading and asked the questions. She was a lifelong student of metaphysics herself. She understood the nature of Akashic readings, and I think she understood both their potentials and their limitations. Not everyone who studies readings does.

When we begin to study readings we are, honestly, dazzled; both by the extraordinary information and by the beauty we encounter, especially in uncovering the work of the karmic weavers. They not only work directly on our auras, but also reach into day to day reality to cause us to meet the people and the lessons we need to grow. They bring gifts as well, and we'll read more about that later. These are gifts of healing, of talents remembered, and energy to realize our prayers.

Truly they work from spirit to unfold our soul plans according to the truths of the Akashic Record. Both the complexity of that work, and its endurance over time, are simply too much for us to grasp. They literally weave into the auras of those involved the qualities needed, and weave out the values that will not serve.

The transcribed reading begins here:

Jill, the conductor here, takes me up the terraces and into the Temple: We are reading for Janet --------------. Janet's grandmother is present. Janet's mother is working in a hospital in the city of ------------.

See before you the altar with its light shining brightly. This is the one light that lights every man and every woman who comes into the world.

Recall this promise: "I will bring to thy remembrance all things, whatsoever you have need of, even from the foundation of the world." Be with us, if you will, Source of our Beings, Creator; healers, physicians and unselfish ones, witness here. Open for us the Book of Life of Janet ------------, born September ---, 1985 in -----------------, Virginia. Draw upon records past, present, and those formed for the future to explain the forces at work in and about this soul and within this body.

Brian: I'm handed this book by a wise, wise man, having white hair and a white beard. As his eyes meet mine, there's something so profound that I cannot find words here, for what I feel in the transmission of this book. The book itself is covered with white lace. I open it, and the records are written in gold script. This cover and its appearance are symbolic of a purpose formed long before Janet was born.

The conductor asks: what is Janet's soul purpose for this lifetime?

Brian: I see gas lamps burning in a hallway with a dark wooden stair. Behind me, there's a carriage, also with gas lamps burning. And we're in a fine home, not a mansion, but a fine home such as might have been occupied by a physician ... and *was* occupied by a physician. We go up this stair, and in a room at the top of the stairs there is a child who is ill. She's about nine. I wait.

As things unfold, I see that this child's name is AUDREY. She's been brought to this physician's home for her life to be saved, if possible. She's nursed in this home for several weeks. Ultimately, she succumbs. But during this time, she learns in an indelible way what selfless service is, and she learns it from this physician, his family and his daughters. The doctor's name is LASSITER.

After she has left this life in 19th century London, Audrey's spirit lingers in this home for years. She integrates this selfless sense of service, along with the loving care that this physician and his family live. And by following the souls of those who come and survive, and those who come and pass, her soul comes to understand that souls can volunteer to enter a family and draw that family together in love.

They find soul values they would not have met, or perceived, or learned, had their lives proceeded along more conventional paths. Janet elected to do that, elected to be born to Sandra, and be profoundly handicapped. She meant to deeply affect the lives of everyone connected to her. In that sense, she has been the author of this family's soul plan in this incarnation. And if you, Sandra, could see her soul, you would see that her soul is in no sense handicapped. The light that shines within her speaks of her unselfish purpose.

But it has not been an easy walk nor an easy set of lessons for those who have cared for her. They have risen to the challenge and grown in love and unselfishness, and especially in understanding what it means to be born a person not quite equal in life. That was Janet's purpose.

Her condition is in no sense an accident, although there have been questions about that. But her conception, her gestation, her birth, and her early years were closely supervised from spirit to bring about this life exactly as she has lived it.

If we could see this life with the eyes of our souls, truly we would be overcome with admiration at the unselfishness that led to this plan, and the unselfishness that has been expressed in its execution.

Let's look ahead to the long term. Janet is satisfied that she has accomplished what she came to do. She is ready for the burden of her care to be lifted here. It has worked in those lives what it was meant to work. So let's look at those details.

How shall we put this? I see an image here and I'll have to unfold it. I'm seeing the white clay pipe of the Scots-Irish people who came to this continent and to this Tidewater area of Virginia, in most cases as indentured servants.

Sandra, you came here too, in a former life as an indentured servant. That was a difficult life, as the life of most such servants was difficult. We would say simply that Sandra, as the woman she was then, stuck it out. She served her entire term of indenture.

Truly what was asked of her then was too much. And what it brought to that woman, whose name then we see was ELIZABETH AHERNE, was a wave of bitterness. Bitterness at the way she had been used, and bitterness at the injustice of the indenture system.

So while she was used to raise children, and to bear that load; and care for the sick, and tend the house, and cook; it all brought about a bitter reaction in her soul. But in this life, she's handled those same tasks with love that she's renewed over and over, with prayer, with her mother love, with her practice as a nurse. All that bitterness has been washed away from her soul. She is beautiful in every way.

We trust that she will hear, in my words and in my voice, and in Jill's voice, and in Grandmother's voice too, our understanding of this process, which we three have all seen before. It isn't always like this. Not every handicapped child has come to do an Angel's job, but many have. Not every child who suffers from a terrible disease has willingly volunteered for it, but most have.

Here is a principle that we often see. It is not meant as a generality to be spoken to the parent of a handicapped child. No one I have known in twenty-five years as a school psychologist would have taken comfort from the principle alone.

Truly the parent who needs to apply that principle has to meet it inside, in images that ring in the soul, in dreams that call up the memories with all the specifics, just as Nora in chapter 2 had to re-encounter images from far memories in order to grasp the reactions in her own soul. Meditation and prayer bring these things to light gradually, day by day, as they must be met to give their gifts of new energy.

Conductor: Janet has been having symptoms of Obsessive-Compulsive Disorder, and she is unable to vocalize what is bothering her. What is the underlying cause? How can we help her, whether with medication or otherwise? … and our last question is about the long-term outlook.

Brian: Obsessive-compulsive disorder is written in the physical structure of the brain. It's not a soul pattern, nor does it originate in deep consciousness.

It's literally written in the cells, in the pathways, and in the nervous signals of the brain. Its nature is such that as a body survives into adult years and beyond, it usually grows worse. That's what's happening with Janet.

It's a picture then of brain cells unable to make sense of the daily challenges, dropping back into a well-worn and practiced pattern, so that in consciousness she cannot separate what's important and what is real from what continually reasserts itself, literally in a feedback loop.

The medications that have been employed are not working very well at this time. Let's look at whether better medications can be found ... well, the medications that are under consideration, and they're intelligently considered, will reduce her functioning in some important ways: in initiative, in the ability to perceive what is being asked of her, and in her ability to remain organized as she meets the requests that are made. But it is time to switch to medications that have that character.

When that change is made, she's going to need more care, and more skilled care, than her mother can provide. And more care and more skilled care than helpers will be able to provide.

Nevertheless, that's what is necessary. Honestly, is acutely necessary. She's going to need to be shifted to a locale that can provide skilled nursing care and what we call occupational therapy. This gradual loss and diminishing function will not be reversed. She will decline. No one can reverse that decline. You might say, Grandmother, it's on the schedule. It's part of the plan.

She draws what she needs out of her caregivers. She draws it out of them as, 'What should I do in the next few minutes?' Her mental references, then, are renewed across an intuitive link. She processes very little the real-life indicators of what is next, what's appropriate, what's expected of her. She really draws that intuitively from her caregivers, especially from mother.

This happens in the immediate, that is to say, she can't plan ahead. It's an *energy transfer*, and that's exhausting for her caregivers, no less for those in the daycare, and no less for mother as Janet quite literally draws from each of them the energy she uses to organize herself for the next thing in the day's schedule.

Her need for that kind of energy and direction will not diminish. Her ability to utilize it will diminish instead.

The medications that are being considered now will help her remain quiescent, not agitated, not anxious, not seeking, seeking, seeking for what she should be doing next, which is the heart of the present problems.

She'll need care to consume her meals. She'll need care for personal hygiene. She'll need care at bedtime. These things are not different in principle from her needs now, but they are different in degree. She'll need guidance much of every day from a person who is practiced at using gestures, language and physical support to help patients do what they need to do for themselves.

She needs the kind of skilled nursing caregivers who can recognize when she's functioning at the right level of medication, and when she's not; when she's tired, and when she is suffering from the little illnesses that we all get, but which impact her more severely. Do you have questions about any of that?

Grandmother: But my daughter is a nurse!

Brian: Yes, she's a nurse, but she's providing for Janet out of her personal energy and her love.

Grandmother: Her mother will know, because she's a nurse. And she will hear what you have to say. But accepting that it's time -- I think that's going to be the hardest thing here.

Brian: That's going to be the hardest thing, yes. And because of her own understanding of medical issues Sandra has known for a long time that this would come. She has not really wanted it to come.

There's a certain amount of denial about what a burden this has become. So let us see what we can give for Sandra. We won't need her birthdate here.

Sandra didn't come by her beauty overnight. She met challenge after challenge and rose to them. She kept her ability to love this girl and made those lessons her own. Do you understand? As Mr. Cayce would have said, she has overcome. Because that's true, Janet's job is done. Today we're not going to go into the other parts of what Janet took on, nor to the other persons she meant to affect.

Grandmother, you didn't have to overcome for Janet's sake. You loved her naturally. You gave to her out of your own *spiritual store*. Do you understand? And despite physical appearances you have been a rock of strength to your daughter. Can you accept that? I hope so. Take yourself off of the hook. You may seem frail to some, but your spirit is not frail.

Grandmother: Oh!

Brian: You've done your part here. Now, how can we help Sandra accept that it's time?

Grandmother: Yeah, that's big.

Well, Sandra's done her job as a human and as a soul, and she's grown. It's time to pass it to those for whom it's a job just as being a nurse is a job. That's a fine job. It's not inhuman at all.

Will Janet be a patient who can be cared for? Yes, she will. Her Angels and her guides will see to it. If we as a family we cannot let go, well, Janet will show more symptoms until we accept it.

She'll experience this change as a less stressful environment, and it *is* a less stressful environment. Those for whom meeting her needs is a professional commitment will not experience the emotions that mother and grandmother and others feel. That will make less stress for Janet.

This is not news to anyone: Janet is supremely sensitive to the emotions of the people around her. That doesn't mean that she's always kind or easy to get along with. No, she's as sensitive as a tambourine, which is the image I'm given here. She sometimes rattles and bangs when the people around her aren't serene. That's part of the assignment that she undertook. She'll settle down in the skilled nursing care facility. She'll rattle and bang a lot less.

So how can we comfort Sandra as she lets go? Does she understand, does Sandra understand, that souls undertake these assignments?

She's ready to understand it, but she hasn't yet. That will take time. What can we give that will help her understand that autistic children, many handicapped children, children who die young, especially from ... oh, the more calamitous diseases ... often accept this assignment before they arrive on earth. They accept it out of love. They experience the journey as a journey of love. And when it is time, they depart from their bodies in peace. So we trust that Sandra will hear this when she listens to this recording.

Here is our promise to Sandra: peace will come. It won't take so long. You both have the experience and the common sense to see the wisdom of this move, but the emotional investment has been great. The emotional bodies, really, Sandra's emotional body, will have to adjust to the change. It will feel like a loss. It will feel like part of her has been removed right through the solar plexus. That will pass. Do you understand?

Grandmother: Yes.

Brian: There is no reason to mourn. Janet will pass her days in peace. We see that she has a pretty strong body. Is that an accurate perception?

Grandmother: Yes.

Brian: Yes, so she's not going to expire next year. She's going to live out her days cheerfully and joyfully, as she prepared to do. She will come to love this facility and the people around her. She will express love to them, and those experienced in this work will recognize it and receive it. I am trying to comfort Sandra with these perceptions, because I see that she will need help to understand.

There is no rush. This is not urgent. If you all walk through it deliberately, you won't make mistakes. You'll come to the end of this process without regrets. Making these changes planfully and intelligently is part of the process.

This life Janet undertook is written indelibly in her body by Janet's own plan. That can be hard for the parent of a handicapped child to accept. But that is usually the plan, and I see quite clearly it was Janet's plan. Now, what can we see or say that will help Sandra see that, if she hasn't seen it already?

I'm seeing a symbol I don't understand, so we'll have to unfold it. I see a white lily, and it's not the lily of death.

Conductor: Resurrection?

Brian: Not the lily of resurrection. It's not a grand concept. The cab that brought the girl Audrey to that doctor's home was owned by her family. It was a Hansom cab. There were always lilies in little side glasses on either side of the carriage. That girl loved those lilies. Every time she got into that carriage, she looked for them. Janet too has loved the flowers and the blossoms around her. It's a loving link to Audrey's life.

Simple as it may seem, it would be good for Sandra to keep blossoms on the kitchen table to remind her that every life is planned. Good to consider the lilies of the field, for "they do not sow, nor do they reap, but Solomon in all his glory was not arrayed as beautifully as these."

So it is with Janet. Hers will continue to be the beautiful life, filled with meaning and love, that she planned.

Conductor: Is there anything more that should or could be given at this time?

Brian: In a matter of only months, she will not think, "I've been abandoned." And of course, she hasn't been abandoned. She'll still see her loved ones.

Grandmother: I've felt for a long time that she came into this life to give love to everybody. She was just pure love. She was always getting people to hug one another.

Brian: Yes. The plan has worked. Janet's plan – AUDREY's plan, more properly --- has worked. And she herself is a soul who didn't have to come back. She chose to come back. This life has been a gift to the members of her family.

Grandmother: That hasn't been that way as much now that ... she changed there.

Brian: Yes. Cognitively, she's slipping. But souls know very well how to withdraw gradually and to spend more and more time in the fields of unconnected memory. That's Janet's plan for her departure from this life. The restlessness she shows now is only the initial stage of that bio- physical process. She will quiet down and she will live for quite a while.

Grandmother: Anything else you could add?

Brian: Let's think about Grandmother for a minute, all right? All your life, you have studied ... I don't want to call them "spiritual laws.""They are really *principles* and *forces*. You have learned how to let them support you in your walk, not how to take comfort from them, but quite literally to draw on the energy which the universal laws put into our beings as they make input into our lives.

That's a bit of an abstract thought put in the only language I've been able to find. But it isn't abstract, and it isn't a concept. Universal Forces and Angels have walked with you. And they'll walk with you through this change too. But intellectually, you understand it, and that eases things a bit.

Don't be sad. Sandra will recover, and soon. She'll enjoy her visits to Janet and know peace. You'll be there to see it. That's a blessing and a promise. And on that note, we'll be through for now.

Grandmother: Thank you.

Conductor: See yourself back in the temple …

Brian: I'm going to mention one thing more. Sandra's name when she was indentured was ELIZABETH AHERNE. Records of her indenture could be found here in the Tidewater area. And records of Doctor Lassiter could also be found in London. Go ahead, Jill.

Conductor: Okay. Let go of all striving now, and release the outcome to those who love and cherish this seeker ...

Grandmother was in her early nineties when this reading was done. She was familiar with the concepts of reincarnation and soul purposes, but Sandra knew less. You can hear the Source of the reading carefully painting a picture that was both human and subject to verification in order to help Sandra's accept what was given here.

And did Sandra accept it? No, not at first. Has she, or will she? I can't be sure. I am told that the reading made a difference in the family, but as so often, time will be required to make that outcome clear.

Given at the Fellowship of the Inner Light
Virginia Beach, Virginia
Conducted by Jill Allbrandt
February, 2018

Doris, A Long Life

Chapter 6

AS I CHOSE SUBJECTS FOR THIS BOOK from among four hundred readings, I set out to give the book a focus on those who felt called to a way of life, or to a spiritual expression that could be placed at the center of a life. In practice I believe these choices are virtually identical to finding your way to your life purpose. I had mostly youthful or midlife choices in mind, but Doris's reading took me in a different direction. Here we look at the life of a woman who overcame, whose life had been outwardly unremarkable, but inwardly quite extraordinary.

Starting in 1936 Doris made her way in the American Midwest. Most of her choices and most of her challenges probably seemed ordinary to her neighbors. But she had an inner life, almost a secret life, that sustained her in a wonderful way. Her joy was tempered by the lifelong alcoholism of her husband, a senior military man, who despite an outwardly successful career never addressed that problem. Nevertheless she uncovered and built on a faith that sustained her and renewed her over and over.

Patti, the conductor here: Servants of the Christ Spirit, open the records to us and guide us, that we may read truly for the wholeness and healing of this woman, her family, and those she came to serve and support in this lifetime. Be present with us, you Witnesses, you who understand Time and the Records and the purposes of the Masters for the Earth at this time. Give us please the Book of Life for Doris -------, born with the name Doris ----------- on the date December ---, 1936, in Indianapolis, Indiana.

Brian: All right, we have this book. It is handed to me by two white-robed teachers, both male. The book itself has a cover. It's covered in white lace, crocheted as white lace gloves were crocheted when Doris was a girl. This cover makes a lovely and a graceful impression. When we open the book, we see first the record of her birth, which was an event both ordinary and extraordinary, and served to draw her family together in a way that lasted for many years. With that purpose, with the meaningfulness of Doris's birth into this family of hers at that particular time, that particular place and no other, as a theme, let's proceed to the questions.

Conductor, reading Doris's question: How far back does it go, that I know what I know now?

Brian: We see first a symbol. It's an ear of corn, and it's not modern corn. It's ancient corn, not much bigger than a grown man's thumb, covered with tiny kernels. This is the crop that was grown in Egypt, an Egypt older than the one of which we have an historical record. That Egypt was transformed by the outflux, the emigration, of the sages from Atlantis. That entire process was not done overnight but happened literally over scores of thousands of years.

We're seeing the corn in the fields around the many little towns in Egypt. Yes, this is the Egypt that figures so strongly in the Edgar Cayce story, not an Egypt of fearsome temples or of great stone gods, but an Egypt that was self-sustaining, and prosperous, and peopled by farmers and a few traders who lived in harmony with each other and with their neighbors. In that Egypt they did not raise great armies, nor did they put great pharaohs on thrones.

Doris lived not one but two lives close together in time in that Egypt. As a child she was raised in the communal houses where children were raised in that time and place. She learned to meditate as naturally as children learn to play and eat and sing, because that was the custom. She learned even by the age of six or seven that there was a light that lived inside her, and that light was her guide in life.

You were born into this life, Doris, knowing that light was there. In that life in Egypt, you never experienced the kinds of conflicts, the kinds of ignorance, or the kinds of violence that prevailed in the countries neighboring Egypt. Doris, you chose to enter this life wanting to experience again that kind of peace, the inner peace too, and that kind of solid understanding of what community is, how people care for each other, how families are made, how such communities contribute to the strength of a nation.

You were born into an Indiana family that was exemplary of the American ideal in that decade of the 1930's when, as the rest of the country struggled to recover from the great Wall Street crash; as the country struggled to understand a nation just starting down the road to industrialization; the American idea was preserved and brought forward by those farming communities in the Midwest, in Indiana, Ohio, Illinois, and Michigan.

You came to be a part of that. You came to be shaped by that value, not by the politics of the day at all, but instead, by the kind of solid identity that children in those communities took in with their milk and their breakfast cereal and their eggs. They knew who they were and what they were here to do. You wanted that as the basis, the foundation for the life that you would live this time. Do you understand?

Doris: Yes. That's quite true, you know.

Brian: Those values were formed in that life in that … we're calling it Egypt, although there's very little in the Egypt of that time that we would think of as Egyptian. That's the way they lived too.

Yes, the soul we think of as Edgar Cayce was not the only leader, but he was one of the leaders. He functioned actually more as a sage than as a king or governor, but one who understood perfectly what it takes to build a community founded on the rhythms of the agricultural year.

He understood perfectly what it takes to irrigate a land like Egypt, and how to turn that soil into productive, sheltering ground for healthy families and healthy communities. He was able to impart that, not to one or two but, we see here, nine generations of Egyptians, who learned that directly from him. Learned from the schools that he oversaw, even from those homes where children were gathered at quite a tender age and schooled in how to be, not just citizens, but good stewards of the Earth and good caretakers to each other. You learned those lessons well.

Neither of your lives in Egypt were long lives. The people in that place and time understood what a healthy life was, but they did succumb to infections. They did succumb at times to toxic water. They did succumb at times to the rigors of the storms and the weather, for both were severe. You came out of those lives understanding and accepting that Earth can be a difficult place to be, but understanding and overjoyed to know that everything on Earth can be managed, even conquered, by people who work together. For this was the heart of the message that Raa Taa, the one we know as Edgar Cayce, taught: that cooperation was the secret of Atlantean life.

He transmitted that to those souls in Egypt, and not to Egypt alone. There were other Atlantean communities in Southeast Asia, South America, Northern Europe, the northern edges of India, and even on some islands and continents that are gone now.

Always and everywhere, the Atlantean message was cooperation. For the leaders of that society rested, not between lives, but rested in underground chambers for 40 and 60 years at a time. They would so replenish and recreate their bodies, and return literally with the same names and the same features over and over, until they lived lives 800 and 900 years long. This is historical fact. That was the source of their wisdom and their understanding. Not aliens, not extraordinary scriptures, not even "the great and terrible crystal," but the kind of wisdom we all accrue when we have long lives and reflect on what we've lived. Do you understand, Doris?

Doris: Yes.

Brian: That *was* the Atlantean treasure. It still is. Now, yes, you came this time into an agricultural community centered around corn and wheat and animal husbandry, in a place that weathered that Great Depression. That community paid the price for the two world wars, and came through with their culture and their values not only intact, but strengthened. They did not succumb to the violence nor to the racial hatreds that were stored up in those wars. They did not succumb to the anger that all decent people in every nation felt toward those who started those wars. Those people in the American Midwest kept their eyes fixed on healthy families in healthy towns, with a healthy relationship to Earth and to God.

They did see God not as the lord of heaven and hell, but as a force that caused the sun to shine and the crops to grow and the children to grow up straight and strong. Do you understand?

Doris: Yes.

Brian: All right. You've lived those values. Those have been your values, not really so fashionable for much of your life, but good values, and you've transmitted them, and not just to your own family either. I think we're ready for that next question.

Conductor, reading Doris's question: What does Edgar Cayce and his example mean to my soul?

I am seeing a single stalk of a green grass. It has come through the earth, and it's grown tall, but it's still folded, and now it's unfolding before me.

Edgar Cayce's example has lived in your soul and has been renewed and made perfect every springtime of your life. As a soul, as an individual soul, the great lesson of his life as Edgar Cayce, the great lesson of his life as Raa Taa too, was to let go of the wrongs and hurts of defeats, to rise up again and again as new as springtime, and give what he had to give.

It was a simple philosophy. It's not a very American philosophy to let go of wrongs and hurts, never to dwell on vengeance, resentment, never to set out to get even, always ready to be reconciled; to start fresh in family life, in community life, with God, too.

He did this even though his soul lived its dark times in both of those existences. For him, the question was not, "Is there a God, and is he good?" For him, the question was, "I know there's a God. Am I good enough to walk with Him?" He answered that question yes in both lives.

He saw plenty of hardship in both lives, plenty of rejection and disappointment and yet renewed himself in ... this idea is hard to put into words ... in this value. In his soul, he knew and made his own, that he was good enough to walk with God, good enough to take part in God's creation. Even though in both lives he saw his own failures clearly, even though in both lives he punished himself severely, judged himself for having disappointed and let down those who loved him the most and were closest to him. Nevertheless, it never quite overcame him in either life. Over and over, he stood up again and again and said, "Yes, I am a Son of God, and yes, I will turn my hand to God's creation, and if and when I fail, I'll let it go and do it again."

Do you understand, Doris?

Doris: Yes, that's wonderful.

Brian: Yes. That's been your value, too. That's what you wanted. That's what you came to do. It's not a philosophy. It's been an experience for you to pick up, to start again, even to hold this hope, this belief, this wonderful secret inside for the years at a time that you had to do that. Do you understand?

Doris: Yes.

Brian: That was a challenge, Doris. You came to a place and a time and even to a family where women's opinions on cooking and child rearing and the care of the sick were sought and valued. You came to a family where the understanding of medical science was sought and valued, but you lived in a time and in a culture where women's opinions in general were not welcome. Do you understand?

Doris: Yes.

Brian: You've lived through the change in this country about that.

Doris: Yes, it was happening all the time. Except my mother would keep telling me it would change in time, that even though when I was quite young I could see that none of the women were involved in politics or any of these situations you have mentioned. Somehow, I knew, though, that things would improve as I grew older, and someday, I would be on my own. I really started believing in reincarnation as soon as I heard about Edgar Cayce. I knew that I would be back again and again, and we would all be together.

Brian: Yes, you came with a grasp on all the truths of the soul. You recognized them instantly whenever they were presented, more or less laid in your path. You knew, and you claimed them for your own, and you've lived them. Now, let us look at this moment, and see if there are other incarnations that have mattered a great deal in your life this time.

Doris: I would say especially great masters like Dwaj Kul, Saint Germain, all of the great masters from India, Paramahansa Yogananda too. I was driven to finish his book. It just took me a very long time. I wanted to know all about him and then I took a correspondence course for two to three years all about his theories. I would receive lessons each month. I'd lived in Minnesota at the time, for about 12 years.

I thought it was so wonderful about the yogic techniques. Again, it was all kept inside me, but this time, I felt strong, and it made no difference that most of the people in my neighborhood did not understand me, that I was learning to be strong and not worry about it.

Brian: You did grow stronger. There were two lives that influenced you here. The first life was in India, where you learned this Ancient Wisdom at the feet of teachers of Sanskrit. You were of gentle birth, not a queen in that life, but it was a life without hardships. You had a fine mind and the leisure to pursue these studies, but you really lived a life of so little conflict that there came a time between lives when you said, "I'm not sure I could live this way on Earth, knowing these things and seeing the gap between the world as it is and these truths that I understand."

So you had an incarnation ... try to see this: you were a queen. You were queen of a country in northern Europe, a Scandinavian country, early in the 17th century. You were well-educated, which was rare in any strata of society and, you might be surprised to hear, equally rare among royal families. You recognized these ancient truths in the form they presented themselves in your life, coming to your country during the Renaissance. You sought those who knew the real origins.

In that life, Doris, you literally took off white ermine robes and disguised yourself as an ordinary young woman of what we would call the middle class, or the bourgeoisie, and sought out the Gypsy women. They were not respectable. They were persecuted, but they knew these truths. You sought them out, and you asked them good questions that caused them to share their wisdom with you. They brought to mind again all that you had learned in that life in India, which was, we would say today, *highly esoteric*.

The orders of the universe, the paths of the masters, the hierarchies, human, angelic, and otherwise — these memories came back to you, spurred by the wisdom that the Gypsies shared. Once again, however, you could speak these truths to very, very few. You gathered about yourself a band ... what are these women called? Not maids and not servants ... young women of gentle birth, or at least gentle upbringing … ah, "Ladies in Waiting."

You shared those truths with those ladies in waiting and additionally made their lives so fair, so lovely really, that you won their love and you've kept their love down through the ages. You could not speak these truths to the men in your life.

Doris: That's true.

Brian: They knew too much.

Conductor: At least they thought they did!

Brian: They knew about armies, and crowns, and successions, and all of that. You shared what you knew with those ladies in waiting, who had quite humble jobs. They were dressers. They were launderers. They prepared you for court appearances, you see, but they were not ignorant, nor were they servants or slaves. You loved them, and they loved you. Doris, one of them came back as your daughter.

Doris: That must be Jennifer. I have only one daughter.

Brian: She came back to experience again what I would have to call your gentle, loving concern, your willingness to involve yourself in her life and circumstances. Though in that life she was very, very far from you in social rank and wealth, you cared, and it mattered to her. She came back quite literally to bask in that love from you again. Do you understand?

Doris: Yes. That is wonderful. You are 100% correct. From the moment she took her first breath, there was some difficulty, and yet she constantly progressed. I was very involved with her. It was wonderful to see how even though she was struggling so in school, I knew that I could help her, that somehow, she would get by and have the right teachers. I was able to do this even though she was in the middle of our two sons. They were so kind to her, as was Jim. Now, I even told a few of my friends this past week how Jennifer is so much on her own now.

Brian: We see that you understand the very best parts of it. You did surround her, not just with protection but with understanding love. You did prevail over conditions which were not hostile but were in many ways indifferent to her success.

Doris: Thank you for reminding me of all of that.

Brian: Let's see if there were other lives that have been a

foundation or a steppingstone for you in this one. We are seeing another life in another European court, not as a queen, but as the wife of a noble, a leader of soldiers.

In that life, you learned how to value a man who protected the people who looked to him for protection. This gave you sufficient depth of understanding to live with Jim and to respect his choice of profession. Truly, you came to understand that there are dangerous and violent forces, that we do need men of strength. You learned it even though in that life and in this one, yes, those men of strength were often sent to conflicts that were unnecessary and at times unjust, but it gave you sufficient strength to support your husband this time.

He was your husband that time, too. Unlike the stereotype that we see in movies, he was not a violent or abrupt man who abused power routinely because he was born to it. He was instead a responsible man who had some appreciation for those who served him. We don't mean that he was in any sense democratic or in any sense soft on the people who served him, no, but he respected their integrity and the jobs that they did. He did his best, we would say, to spend those resources wisely. Do you understand?

Doris: Yes. Jim was quite musical, and it was beautiful to hear him sing or play. He could do all of this by ear. He didn't need any lessons. It was very helpful to me to see this other side of him even though I knew, as you were telling me about Scandinavia … we were in Wisconsin for 25 years because of the home office where he chose to work, and it was cold there, and yet we survived beautifully with the extreme cold. Most of our friends were Scandinavians. Somehow, we made it through a lot of that.

It's not finished as far as what I'm going through now. He's still really questioning me, and I feel it's a jealous feeling that deep down, he knows I have all of these wonderful experiences since the time I started with Edgar Cayce's teachings. He is curious, and I help him along if he seems to want to make another trip to Virginia Beach. It's a challenge.

Brian: Let's take a brief look at that … he enjoyed that Wisconsin time, and he enjoys not only that culture but that climate. It does remind him of what really was quite a noble life, when he was in Scandinavia with you. Now, how can you ease his mind and your relationship with him? That may be the most telling way to put this question.

Doris: The biggest difficulty ... it's huge. I work on it daily. It's getting worse. It's the severe alcoholism. My father was identical. I ask myself, as I did years ago, why didn't I pick up on this in college when I met him? I don't want to blame myself, but there's still the dilemma. He's trying, but it's getting worse. After all … he is 80 now, and it's …

Brian: We see here that it's late. It's late. What can we offer? First words I'm given are, 'Don't struggle.' Hard as it is, it's been his lesson. Within himself, he's entirely aware that this weakness of his has cost you dearly, and cost the two of you as a couple too. According to what we see here, what these teachers are telling me, he will sort that out when this life has ended. They say he will never take this path again. It has been your ... honestly, this may not feel good. It has been your tenderness and your gentleness, more than your corrections or complaints or efforts, that will cause him to, I guess the word is, repent, but it will not happen while he's in this body and this life.

You can know some peace if you will release that and literally, Doris, pray for his afterlife. It is in place. It is designed. It will work, as these things go, rather swiftly for him. He has walked the entire journey to completion. He will see it whole when he is freed from this body with its conditioning, with its dependence on this chemical. Do you understand?

Doris: Mm-hmm. Yes.

Brian: He will not be able to get free while he's in this body. That's not good news, but it's probably not surprising news. You can find relief if you will pray for the experiences that will come to him when he leaves this body for good. I'm told you will glimpse them even now, if you pray to see them, and that will give you some peace. Do you understand?

Doris: Yes. I have felt quite an increasing change in him during the last year or so. I can almost see and feel the sorrow, and yet just a year or two ago, he was elected to be chairman of the board of a counseling center that spun off from a church. He enjoyed that very much. He was very religious for a long while and had been asked to take this position. I know he's torn now between the two. The church didn't have enough money to keep it going.

I just watch and notice that he is enjoying being with male friends. Unfortunately, they are not too different from the kind of person that he is now. He is struggling. He was pleased to drive me here tonight, yet I could feel that he knew he couldn't be involved at the same time, that he's just too …

Brian: He can't change, you see. His conscience has never been extinguished. You must know that about him. Of course, he would face humiliating truths in a situation like 'this reading. Do you understand?

Doris: Yes.

Brian: Yes, the counseling center meant a lot to him, and yes, the activities in which he will take part when he's gone from this body will be quite like those. He will draw on strengths that he did not build but only glimpsed there. More than either of those things, he will draw on your example.

He knows inside himself what a price he's paid. The only lesson left for you is to step back and bless him and let him learn and grow. It's been your burden, but his lesson. Do you understand?

Doris: Yes.

Brian: We know it's difficult to hear.

Doris: It's not that I'm feeling I must be with him again in another life. I don't know that I could take that again the second time. Again, my father was the same way.

Brian: We don't see any such plan. You have paid your dues, and we don't have time left to go into why you elected to face this with your father and your husband, but you did. We all do elect the trials in our lives, I want to say, quite precisely.

In this life, goodness, you have grown a great deal of patience, Doris, a great deal of patience! Should you come back again, such patience will not be required. Such a breast full of beautiful things whose expression is limited will not be your lot again. Do you understand?

Doris: Yes. I was so pleased to hear about my two lives in Egypt. I really felt that, it was amazing.

Brian: We're going to say one more thing about those lives. Know that your true grasp of the esoteric wisdom, truths, the Esoteric Order of Creation, is second to none, because you lived and drew upon it in your personal life this time. Do we have another question?

Conductor: We do. (Reading Doris's question) "Tell me what I need to know most about my own soul."

Brian: All right, this is different ... I see a snowflake, a single crystal, and unmistakably a crystal. Your soul rings like a crystal, rings with a musical sound, and it will ring through the ages.

You have pared away all that was less than true in this existence. It has fallen away from you. You'll go forth from this existence with that kind of crystalline purity. You earned it one year at a time.

You no longer have at any level beliefs that will hold you back or, especially, loyalties and allegiances to ideas that are half-truths. Do you understand that difference? What you'll leave this life with is 100% true, and you've made it 100% your own. That's why this snow crystal represents a ringing purity. It's almost like a poem. Your soul no longer has any ideas and or convictions that are less than true. You will live these truths. They will ring forth from you wherever you go next. Do you understand?

Doris: Mm-hmm. That's just wonderful.

Brian: In heaven or on earth, if you choose to come back, you won't have to hold it inside again. You've made it pure.

Doris: Good. I feel I will come back being able to teach those who have walked in my shoes.

Brian: You would, if you choose to come back. It's not required, not of you. Now I am seeing a line of Teachers. They are teachers of Ancient Wisdom, but they wear no symbols, no hoods, no robes. Their hands are not empty, but free. They welcome you to their company.

This is a spiritual truth: if you began your teachings today, what you would teach would be true. There would be no alloy of the expedient, of superstition, of tradition in what you taught. That's what they're telling me. That's what you'll take from this life when you leave it. They'll be there to meet you, and that's a blessing and a promise.

Given in Florida
March, 2015
Conducted by Patti Phillips
Doris was present

Baker and Ned, PTSD and Cancer

Chapter 7

"BAKER IS A SWEETHEART," Patti said to me when she came to ask me to help Baker. "He takes care of Ned like a mother would. Ned really has to be cared for like a child." Baker and Ned had been partners for twenty-five years. Ned's balance, his walking, and even his thinking were quite impaired after a stroke. Baker himself was a Navy veteran of Viet Nam who had served in the Seabees. He had chosen to have his friends call him Baker every since his years in the service.

Patti told me that Baker had just been diagnosed with a stage IV cancer of the throat, a very aggressive form, and he was headed for a regional cancer center in the north of the state. He had already been to a local cancer specialist and to the VA seeking a better--that is, more optimistic--diagnosis. Patti said, "He will be hospitalized for at least a week and first they are going to pull out all of his teeth."

Baker had been told that the lesion on his tongue was the start of things, but the cancer had already metastasized to his throat. She went on to say that Baker was terrified, especially about the teeth and about the extensive radical surgery that was discussed from the first. Most of all Baker feared that the stress would destabilize him. Baker was sixty-six at this time, and after his Viet Nam days he had had quite a hard time with Post Traumatic Stress Disorder. "A couple of mental hospitalizations," Patti said about this. She also told me, "He is a really faithful Catholic and he prays for everybody in his rehab."

I had talked casually with Baker about many things, but the proposal for a reading was a first. I didn't persuade him. I simply gave him a couple of readings to think about. I told him that if he wanted to take this route I would feel honored to do a reading for him.

When he came for his reading on a Sunday afternoon he brought Ned with him. "Don't worry about Ned," Baker said, "he won't follow any of this." I wasn't sure of that, that but I decided to trust Baker and we went ahead, settling onto sofas in the sunroom of my home in late afternoon light. Patti conducted, seated at my head, while I settled on the floor. Ned and Baker sat together on a small sofa and held hands.

As I do with every seeker, I invited Baker to listen closely and come along in his own mind as I mentally went to the meadow, climbed the terraced mountain with its gardens, and entered the temple on the summit. Baker was no occultist, of course, so chakras and their colors were wholly unknown to him. But as many do, he intuitively joined in, and his attention was complete. That is all it takes to turn on one's subtle senses and become sensitive to the changes that occur as we climb and let the colors act on us. So I believe Baker apprehended what was given in the reading with his own heightened intuitive senses. That is what the seven terraces and the temple were designed to do.

As we began Baker's reading, Patti first spoke our prayer, and this is typical of the way I pray before every reading:

> "Light of life, reveal yourself here today. Unselfish ones, healers, witnesses, be with us we pray. Open the record to us and guide us that we may read truly for the wholeness and the healing of this man, this body, this soul. Draw upon records past, present, and those formed for the future, to explain the forces at work in and about this soul. As you consider the ills of his body, consider his chosen purposes for this incarnation, his deep beliefs, and the choices in front of him."

When we reached Baker's Book of Life, it was a large book, navy blue, and bound in a cover of silver worked in a filigree pattern. As I always do I spoke my impressions of the book before we got to specifics. These impressions serve as the opening notes of a symphony, sounding one or more themes that will be developed as we expand what we see.

Brian begins to speak: We see the kind of filigree you might see decorating the porch on an old Victorian home in Massachusetts, but silver here, not wood. This cover is emblematic of a life designed around old-fashioned values of loyalty and family, love of country, and loyalty to community.

Conductor: Baker has been diagnosed with cancer at the base of his tongue and lymph nodes. What is the truth of this diagnosis, and what are the remedies for body, mind and spirit?

Brian: Let's begin by scanning this site in the body, starting with the crown of the head. We are seeing a healthy brain with good circulation. A brain, we must say, untouched by age, and clear. A brain that has always reasoned clearly and in those periods when emotions undermined clear thinking and reasonable decisions, the problem did not originate in this brain, but originated in that place where emotions are stored and processed and compared, which is the solar plexus. In the abdomen and the body, that's where this activity occurs. We'll mention this again as we come to it.

Looking at the throat, looking at the bronchi, the sinuses, the tongue itself: all right, we are seeing some cancerous cells; we are not seeing a large tumor here. We are looking at a mass that has metastasized, yes, but not severely.

This cancer has received a severe diagnosis because it's a quick growing cancer of an aggressive form, but at this point, let's use the simple language. It has scattered seeds into the soft tissue at the back of the throat, into the lymph nodes and soft tissue structures on either side of the throat, and to a tiny extent, into the gums. None of these sites is exhibiting a frank tumor to this scan at this time. They are located in very swiftly-growing tissues of the body, however, but are also located in some of the body tissues that heal fastest, faster almost than any other tissue in the body, under normal circumstances.

I'm looking at the bronchus and the bronchi, the tubes that transmit air to the upper reaches of the lungs, and we are seeing some inflammation there, not cancer related. The body shows that throughout this life, this man has had this bronchial inflammation, largely due the fumes of automotive exhaust. This has rendered this entire throat and upper chest vulnerable to infection, to a certain degree. I don't want to call it a disease condition, but a compromised condition. That has been -- not the largest contributor, not exactly a cause -- but a contributor to this cancerous condition that has developed. Not aggravated by substances ingested, neither by food nor by tobacco, nor by any other substances that have left a record in this part of the body.

I'm looking at the heart and the respiratory center, that plexus of nerves and glands that control the heart and respiratory system together, from a single site just under the sternum, the flat bone at the front of the chest. How does this look? The respiratory center is physically strong in Baker's body. Baker's sternum is unusually sensitive to emotions, so that at times breathing itself has been eclipsed by strong emotions. Also, the confidence that emanates from the respiratory center throughout the body has at times been eclipsed by strong emotions that originate right here, in the heart center. Let's digress from this cancer for a moment to talk about that.

If we were to use language that everyone in the family would understand, we would have to say that Baker is a man who has seen too much, too much of violence.

Baker has been a man never attracted to violent men, nor to men who have in this life, for whatever reason, trained themselves to be killers, in or out of uniform. Baker came into this life with a purpose to support family, with a purpose to support community, to live a generous spirit toward all of mankind. He came to enter into family in a community where old divisions of belief, tradition, race, and religion just barely supported his soul's purpose. So there has been, to use a little more unusual language, a struggle and a pain in the heart center from the earliest years of Baker's life.

He's overcome it again and again but he was never a man fashioned to slash his way through life, neither with a sword nor with a bulldozer. He's been honorable. This of course is not a handicap.

Baker's love for those he has loved, and for the communities where he's lived, has come from the heart, not from the solar plexus, Not from a sense of possession, not from a sense of, "This I must defend because it's mine." It always flowed from a heart that wanted the best for everyone in every situation, especially in conflict situations.

He's been a peacekeeper, and has paid the price for trying to bring peace at times in situations where peace was not within reach. Baker, do you understand this?

Baker: Yes.

Brian: All right. Well, Baker, it's made you physically vulnerable, but you are honored by those spirits gathered here, most especially by your parents. It was their dearest prayer to bring such a soul into the family circle.

Coming back now to this diagnosis: we don't see cancer in the bones, the connective tissue, or the muscles. We don't see cancer in this stomach although we do see a stomach that is vulnerable, and always has been, in part to airborne pollutants, and in part to the things we put into our stomachs in a 20th century diet. Baker has known this and has eaten with care, mostly.

Baker, we see that you are vulnerable to a gourmet meal, and your body hasn't always enjoyed that, but it hasn't really affected your health.

We're not seeing metastasized cancer anywhere in this digestive system, nor do we see metastasized cancer in that whole area that we think of as the abdominal sac, which holds all the organs. This cancer is confined to the uppermost areas of the body.

Now we're checking the lymph nodes, the armpits, and under the jaw. Baker, the armpits are clear. These glands under the jaw do have some "seeds" and they are not tumors, but they have some seeds. It would be surprising if they hadn't. The lymph system and the endocrine system throughout this area of the body is a sensitive, totally interconnected system.

All right, let's look to remedies. I have some physicians here now who are looking at the tests that have been done so far, and they are looking directly into your body, Baker. There are several therapeutic methods under discussion here, and I'm being given advice here that I will have to phrase carefully. There is a discussion here of therapy utilizing radium.

Baker, that's an old-fashioned therapy. There's a preference among these physicians for radium, administered through chemistry, that is, using a chemotherapy that's radium-based, and as the primary mode of therapy, instead of radiation applied by an instrument focused in a laser-like fashion. They favor it more than surgery.

Of course, these physicians recognize full well that you won't be in the driver's seat as these discussions are held in the hospital. But Baker, if radium is offered to you as one of the alternatives, that is the recommendation from here, do you understand?

Baker: Yes.

Brian: All right. Radium is a volatile substance, but well understood by the physicians who use it, thanks to sixty years of experience. It less destructive to healthy tissue than virtually all the other chemotherapies. Typically it's implanted in a pellet and then removed after time, a process that's very well understood, and that would be the ideal therapy here.

Now, a second point: they say one of the more difficult parts of the therapy for you, Baker, in your body, will be the ingestion of a balanced diet for the duration of this therapy. It won't be easy.

The recommendation here is a simple one, starting with a six-ounce glass of milk mixed with an egg and with a tablespoon of blackstrap molasses. Take that for breakfast in the morning whenever you are having a diet that is under your own control. That will furnish iron; it will furnish fat in the form of milk and fat, which your body handles well; and it will furnish protein. The combination of the egg and the milk together will furnish protein, and the blackstrap molasses will furnish a whole spectrum of B vitamins. It is B vitamins that are destroyed by radiation therapy and by chemotherapy as well. Do you understand?

Baker: I believe so.

Brian: All right, that simple measure will provide a foundation of nutrition even if you find yourself unable to chew or unable to swallow without discomfort, which is likely to go on for some weeks. What else?

We're seeing vitamins D and E. You do want to fortify yourself before you go into a medical setting. Probably 400 to 800 units daily of vitamin E, taken in capsule form, and derived from wheat germ oil, not from irradiated ergosterol, but wheat germ oil; and vitamin D, also from wheat sources. And for everyone facing therapies with side effects, about a gram a day of vitamin C, probably taken 500 milligrams in the morning and 500 milligrams in the evening, is a good idea.

Looking now at how the body will cope … significant surgeries will be required here, being mindful that the radium therapy would require less. Baker, we're looking now at your soul's experience with surgery over a number of lives. Bodies heal quickly from surgery when the mind is optimistic and so to speak, uncomplicated. Children and dogs heal quickly from surgery, optimists and athletes heal quickly from surgery. Baker, that's not you, so much.

We are looking at those measures which will keep your mind focused in a positive way, and honestly, worry-free. You have a stronger body than you think, but we must say, you have been vulnerable to worry and you have some bad habits in this department. Baker, do you understand?

Baker: Yes.

Brian: All right, so the recommendation is, take your earphones to the hospital, and your CD player or your MP3 player. Bring collections of your favorite tunes and collections of light classics and occupy your mind with music, rather than with television or with talk, and especially not with worry. Do you understand?

Baker: Yes.

Brian: All right. It may seem like a small matter, but Baker, it's not a small matter to your soul in this body. Cancer is an enemy. You will recover more quickly if you banish worry, your other great enemy in this life.

At this point the direction of the reading changed and attention was directed to Baker's Post Traumatic Stress Disorder, particularly to the patterns in Baker's individual soul and to his war history that more or less invited this condition, which was not seen here as mental illness, but more as a profile of motives and beliefs. These were not deficient or flawed in themselves but they were no fit for a war zone.

Brian: Now we're going to take a detour for a minute, Baker. You've been through some hard times emotionally, not solely because of what you've seen in this life. Not solely because of your service in the Viet Nam years either. But also because of the soul memories called up deep below consciousness, as you contemplated the risks and the injuries and the fates of the men around you in your time in the service. Do you understand?

Baker: Mm-hmm. Yes.

Brian: Baker, we are going to put this simply: selfish men do better under the stress of combat. You are anything but selfish. You worried about every man you knew. You felt the fear, the pain, and if you can believe it, the coming injuries to every sensitive, good man's face that you saw. Do you understand?

Baker: Mm-hmm. Yes, I get it.

Brian: You carried all that on your back and you were unable to speak. I know you tend to say very little about it, but that's not an adequate way to put this. Far less than one percent of what you saw, you were able to speak. You held it back, you did not speak, do you understand?

Baker: Yes.

Brian: You were not surrounded by understanding men. On the contrary, you were surrounded by young men pretending not to be afraid. Do you understand that?

Baker: Yes.

Brian: You knew what they were going through, you knew what their real feelings were, and you were dying to speak these things. It was not acceptable. That does not need to be explained to you, does it?

Baker: No.

All right, that's what burdened this throat, more than the chemicals, more than the pollutants. It's carrying those men's pain and fear, and having no place, no listening ear to speak it to. You wanted to comfort them. You wanted to pray with them, but that was, we would say today, "socially unacceptable" in that setting. Do you understand?

Baker: Oh, yes.

Brian: All right, in that sense Baker, you were an unmarked priest to those men. You did comfort them. Many knew that you cared, but young men don't know how to express those perceptions. We know that you understand that. Baker, in your times of prayer in this next week or two … I'm going to use some unusual language.

I want you to take yourself to a chapel that you construct in your own mind, and there bless every man that you remember. Pray for each man, pray for his injuries, pray for the invisible scars that every warrior carries. Pray for those who did not come home, bless them too. Shed tears if you find tears to shed. Do you understand?

Baker: Yes.

Brian: You will clear this area. You will clear this entire area of that unspoken burden you carry -- how can I say this?

You carried a full chaplain's load, but you were not in a position to use a chaplain's tools. So it lodged in here (pointing to throat) and some of it is still there. Pray for them. Bless them. Know that this is real and that it matters. Be now the chaplain you could not be then — this is the very best way you can turn this process around and reinforce your own strengths for the therapeutic measures that are about to be applied.

You'll be your own healer, but you will not be alone. Baker, you've never been alone. We've all been told that you've got to be a saint to see Angels. Baker, that's untrue. We hear them, we see them out of the corners of our eyes, they send us to our friends in need, they give us the tender words we need; and they fit those words to the situation as it really exists.

You came to do this. You came to love men, no shame in that, we all come to love our fellow humans. Your ability to love men and to be a true man in that situation was a gift you asked for, and it was given before you came here. Do you understand?

Baker: Mm-hmm. I sure do.

Brian: All right. You've used that gift well, Baker, depend on that. You've been a good man.

Now how else to prepare for this hospitalization? Baker, I'm seeing Jello! You should have some Jello every day. It absorbs toxins, toxins in the bowel; and Baker, the toxins of fear and worry, do you `understand?

Baker: Mm-hmm, yeah.

Brian: Jello is full of pectin. That's what makes it jell. Pectin absorbs toxins. Now ideally, you'll buy plain Knox Gelatin, make it with apple juice or cherry juice or blueberry juice, but you can buy Jello and you'll do almost as well with the Jello that comes in the package and prepares in five minutes, do you understand?

Baker: Mm-hmm. Yeah.

Brian: I want you to have Jello everyday. It will help very much to clear toxins. Now, what else? Well, we see our herbal remedies, but Baker, their action is slow, and they depend largely on your relationship to the herbal practitioner. We don't really have time to put those things in place here. What else? All right, this will also be for you, and you alone, Baker. Do you have a family Bible?

Baker: Yes.

Brian: I want you to spend 15 minutes each day with that family Bible held right here (just below the heart), just as you already know how to do, and pray for every member of your family that ever judged you, or questioned you, or made distance. Forgive them and bathe them in God's love, and do all those things which we would love to do around the deathbed -- if our heads were clear, if our emotions were good, and we were still in good relationships with those people. But that's very few, Baker. Clear the decks with family, exactly as you know how to do, do you understand? You want to enter into these treatments and this surgery with no regrets, and no unfinished business with family, all right?

Baker: Hm. So, whipped cream on the Jello?

Brian: Whipped cream on the Jello, good idea! All right, we see the inner man coming out, all right! These recommendations are simple, but Baker, they'll put you in charge of the process and that is a place where you need to be. The hospital, the surgery, these are scary places, these are places where no one feels like a tall person, no one feels in charge. Get yourself in charge through these simple measures. Patti, let's go on to question two.

Conductor: Baker is concerned about his responsibility for Ned. What can be given that will help him meet that responsibility in the best way?

Brian: Well, this first, Baker, your union is blessed. You two have your Angels and your guiding spirits. They've been on this question for quite some time. They will be with Ned and they will be … no, let's put this simply. They'll be guarding his emotions as carefully as you have, do you understand that?

Baker: I think so.

Brian: All right. They will be whispering in the ears of those caretakers and Ned will continue to be protected carefully, lovingly. Can these persons do the kind of a job that you have done? Well, no. But an adequate job, yes. And there's been a lot of action around this.

There's actually been a year or more of preparation. In your seeking and in your arrangements, you have not been entirely on your own. That support is going to be there.

Now, we come to the difficult part. Baker, should you succumb to this disease, a way of escape has been prepared for Ned. And let us be frank, Baker. Let us say a parachute has been packed, do you understand?

Baker: Oh, boy.

Brian: So that should Ned find himself alone, he will also find himself on a short, smooth track to an easy exit. Baker, that is the best outcome for him, do you understand?

Baker: Do you see me succumbing to this disease?

Brian: Well, we'll look at that question in a minute. Take a minute, Baker. Right now, we are still dealing with Ned, because half, at least half, of the emotional component here is, "Who will take care of Ned?" Well, the very best planners and helpers in the universe have a good plan here.

Now let's look, Baker, at your own "let's-be-frank" chances.

We have a change. We have a physician and we have a priest. The priest is going to speak first. He says he's already given you advice about your relatives, and he knows them all, living and dead! Second, he says, "Baker, your faith is sufficient to recover. You don't need a Hollywood miracle to recover from this disease. You have your help."

Now the doctor speaks. He says, "You do have substantially better than a 50 percent chance of recovery here." This doctor actually puts it at 70 percent, and he says, "The critical piece is not whether the cancerous cells can be either excised or killed, but whether you can heal the damage from the procedures. Or whether you will become discouraged and say, "I don't want to be here anymore."

Baker, yours is a soul -- this may surprise you -- you don't fear death or the afterlife. You do fear a painful exit. Do you understand that difference?"

Baker: That's true.

Brian: Okay, that's a strength; it's also a bit of a temptation. Now, recovery from this … oh, eighteen months to two years, Baker. That's a long time and there will be pain. Now, you have many times in your private moments, and of course, in your dreams and in your prayers, you have glimpsed, we'll call it the other side; although there are many other sides. It's beautiful to you. You will feel the tug, do you understand?

Baker: Oh yes, I do.

Brian: All right, there's peace there, and no pain, and for one joyful stretch you're not going to be bored! That's good, and that's bad, if we're talking about survival. You'll feel the call to cross over, you'll feel it strongly! And we see … Baker, I'm seeing you at fourteen.

I can't get away from this one, you were a whippersnapper, Baker, and you could drop back into that attitude. You could say, "I'm out of here, kids. I've done everything I wanted to do, I'm out of here!"

Baker: Well, I haven't.

Brian: You haven't. That's right.

Baker: Because I've got to see Ned.

Brian: That's what we see.

Conductor: 10 minutes left.

Ten minutes … and there's more to tell. You've really learned how to live, Baker. You've learned how to enjoy travel, learned how to enjoy a meal, learned how to enjoy the good things in this life. All of that kind of took you by surprise. That fourteen-year-old whippersnapper never dreamed just how rich life could be. Do you understand?

Baker: Yup.

Brian: So we are being told, don't let the whippersnapper pull the ripcord! Prepare in your prayers to make a reasoned, rational choice, Baker, before the pain arrives. Do you understand?

Baker: Yeah.

Brian: Make peace, prepare your exit, or prepare the strength for battle. No one can make this choice for you. Not even these guides, much less this channel. You will very soon realize for yourself that Ned will be taken care of, might even be better taken care of by those who would care for him, in place of a Baker in pain and somewhat disabled himself. We know that you've thought of this, do you understand?

Baker: Yeah. I understand that.

Brian: All right, well, those who care for him thought of it too. The choice is yours; they'll be listening to your prayers.

Baker, you are in charge from this moment on. Make the choice and all of spirit will go to work for the outcome that you choose. Do you understand?

Baker: Yes.

Brian: All right, make it reasonably, Baker. Not with tears. Baker, it isn't sad, there's some pain here, but it is not sad. If you recover from this cancer, if you add to your prayer life, family prayers, prayers for the other veterans you've known, the very young men just like you were, this cancer will not recur. Make that part of your reasoned decision. If you have further questions …

Baker: No, I haven't.

Brian: All right, 70 percent chance of recovery if that's the choice you make. Baker, don't enter into this trial without deciding where you stand. That's the best advice we can give. Patti, further questions?

Conductor: No, I think that's clear.

Brian: All right. Now Baker, there are quite a few people here.

Baker: See my mom and my sister?

Brian: I do. And I see some neighbors, and some classmates, and I see some of the men, not the men who didn't come back from Viet Nam but the men who succumbed later. I've seen your grandparents too, by the way.

Baker, honestly, I'm in a big tall church … I might as well be in your home town in Massachusetts! High ceilings, tall windows. They're with you, Baker. They're going to back you up whatever you choose. They're going to be making music for you in your sedated times. You've got a big team here, Baker. They are ready to bless you. They want the very, very best outcome for you.

Whenever you arrive, they'll be waiting for you with all the love in the world. That is real and it matters. That's a blessing, Baker and with that blessing, we're through for now.

Baker stayed to talk after the reading was done. Ned was present throughout, but sure enough, he didn't really follow. When, after a very few minutes, Baker announced that he had decided to stay, that is, not die, he did it like an umpire calling a pitch. Then Baker, Patti, and I prayed for a while, and off he went. He had his chemo and his radiation -- it was not radium -- but he elected not to have the kind of radical surgery that the oncologists at the regional cancer center recommended.

That all took place seven years ago as I write these words. Today Baker is a vital and a busy man, and just as he planned, making a lovely life with Ned. They have had more than thirty years together now. He is cancer-free and tests well medically but he has lost sixty pounds, and he can't seem to gain despite a diet of gourmet meals that is frankly shocking to me. Every week he sends me Facebook snaps of gorgeous meals and fantastic desserts that he and Ned share in his area's best restaurants. I stopped worrying about him quite a while ago.

Given in Florida
May, 2014
Conducted by Patti Phillips

Gloria, an Analyst

Chapter 8

Gloria was a Freudian analyst, trained by nuns in Brazil, who had come to America in her fifties. She had continued to practice analysis after her move and she brought too her commitments to political activism and to art, for which she was internationally recognized. She had mastered English as well.

I knew that her knowledge of the wellsprings of human nature was vigorous and practical. Her knowledge of esoteric matters was deep as well, and seasoned by years of exploration in her native country. What was new to her in the reading experience was the language of soul growth and the principles of reincarnation.

Long before she came for a reading she had concluded that in some sense she had designed her life. Consequently she had no difficulty accepting that some of the things most of us regard as fate in fact stemmed from her own choices and, somehow, from her truest nature. When in the reading my Source turned to great issues in our lifetimes she was not disconcerted. She already saw herself as part of something larger, and that value underlay her pursuit of social justice.

Gloria conducted her own reading. As we began with the Seven Terraces, I prayed with her, much as I do with most seekers:

Heavenly Father, Divine Mother, be with us. Be mindful of Gloria's purposes, her directions, her choices, her deep roots in this life. Let what is given be given in the language most meaningful to her. Help me leave my own concepts and opinions behind, the better to speak truly what's given here today. Be with us. And thank you for this opportunity. Convey to us please the Book of Life for Gloria ------------------, born on April ---, ---- ,in ----, Brazil.

Brian: We have this book. I haven't seen another like this. It has a cover that's almost lacy, but that lacy cover is carved from ivory. Figures of blossoms, vines, and leaves are cut out and open to the book below, and scattered about the openings are tiny, tiny wildflower blossoms of lavender and blue.

This book is emblematic of a life built around values that are as natural to the earth as those wildflowers, and as little influenced by the place and the culture of this time as wildflowers are. This cover is emblematic too, of the changes that this soul elected to experience. She has worked her way through various creative tasks and projects, finding in each almost a whole new set of values each time she engaged with the work at hand, for this is a soul that comes to every day fresh and new. With that as an overarching theme, let us proceed to the questions.

Gloria: My psychoanalytic practice would require much more reading and study on my part for my practice to truly have a rigorous approach. I enjoy the subject, but also like to dedicate myself to many other aspects of my life. How important is it for the people I see that I deepen my understanding of the psychoanalytical theory? Is there a bigger project to stem from this aspect of myself, or should I feel content with what I'm doing now?

Brian: First we're taken back to the very birth of psychoanalysis, and we see a handful of the finest minds in Europe gathered in Doctor Freud's study. On the desk, on the shelves, and on the tables are lacy doilies and old-fashioned lamps. We also see the figures of ancient gods on these surfaces, some human in form, some animal in form, some both human and animal combined. We see winged beings, and beings with manes, and claws, and tails.

In that atmosphere these men, and later women, came to understand that they had quite literally unearthed an ancient layer of life that went far, far beyond the ideas of Europe and their time. They tapped forces that drew not just their own souls to Europe at that particular time, but also drew the souls of the next several generations. They would come, not to continue history in one long line, but literally to change the entire idea of what a human is; what a mind is; and what are the wellsprings of personality.

They achieved what they set out to achieve, despite the limitations of language, of the society in which they operated, and even the limitations of the associations they created. They unleashed ideas that ripple to this day through many cultures, not just western European-centered culture. They restored to humanity a living relationship with its roots, going back to times long before history, and to societies we have never known, or glimpsed, nor thought of as cultures.

That is Gloria's task as well. That is the tradition she grasped and has continued. It is larger than orthodox practice. That would be an understatement!

For those who come to her she taps the roots of their beings, so dimly reflected in their personal histories -- their narratives and their preoccupations with the challenges and the lessons of their lives. She channels to them not just insight, nor simply advice. She gives them back their heritage wrapped and clothed in her love for them. It lives in them, and they go forth from these therapies mindful not only of the issues they've addressed, but in reality, carrying newly energized connections to their origins as humans. They go forth ready to change the earth and succeeding generations according to the truest values -- not of their minds, nor of their histories -- but of their souls. Yes, quickened by their experience with Gloria.

These things are hinted at in the writings of those early pioneers, circumspect though they were, and required though they were to nod in the direction of respectability. They were required to seem to recognize the limits of medicine as it was understood at the beginning of the 20th century. But in reality, each and every one of those pioneers grasped a different strain of the origins of human nature. That continues to be the case for those who go inside themselves and make of their own narratives a tool bag, a set of myths that they can share with their clients, their patients, and their other connections.

That's your destiny, Gloria. That's what you came to do. Not to be simply a physician of personalities, but a midwife to souls. Not to teach the structure of Freudian theory, but to turn into living things the Sources of their beings in this existence. Not by what you say, but by what you regard and love.

Your love for their histories and their beings is received by these patients, almost all wordlessly. They go forth loving parts of themselves that they did not suspect they had. They would never have admitted these things into consciousness without your help. These are parts which in their own personalities they might see as dark, troubled, limited, even injured. These parts are loved by you because you understand how all of those aspects of their lives have shaped them into the beings they are today, and will for the rest of their walk in the bodies they occupy now.

You did not learn this by theory alone. You bring to the consulting room your love of life. You bring to the consulting room an understanding of the human nature both deep and noble. That's what you came to do.

Do you need more Freudian training to continue this work? Let's look at that question very carefully.

First know that in a previous existence you were one of those pioneers. Know that the pioneer that you were sensed and used therapeutically insights that could never be written, published or spoken in that place and time.

You particularly in that light saw the imminent destruction of most of Europe's superficial accomplishments. You saw the coming of the World Wars. You saw the destruction even of that edifice of truly Germanic culture whose inner-mythic, wild nature emerged and ran wild across the world in World Wars I and II.

You saw it. It would not be accurate to say you were not afraid. You were afraid. You went ahead anyway. You walked through those days, and ultimately, lost your life in one of those Nazi death camps. Nominally, you were Jewish. In reality, quite a skeptic, one not fettered by the heritage of Jewish belief or culture. That did not matter to those who murdered you. Your surname was all that mattered to them.

And so you entered this life never for one minute tempted to reconstruct that great edifice of European culture, the one which embraced war, colonialism, class structure, and inequalities racial, ethnic, and financial. You were done with all of that. That's been true from the day you first drew breath.

So you elected to be born into a culture that literally had no need of its European heritage. A vital culture that rested with one foot in the jungle, and another foot — oh, how should we put this? — in the life and heritage of the Black Africans who created so much of what Brazilian culture is today. Do you understand that?

Gloria: Yes.

Brian: All right. That's where you really stand. European culture has no secrets from you. It also holds very little of your interest. You have wanted to know first-hand the forces that rule the land of your birth. Actually, they are best represented by the great animals of the jungle. Not by the little statuettes, not by the prayers, or the songs, nor even by the visions, but by the forces that stir people to life on that South American continent.

These are the forces that invest themselves in those infants born on that continent. Throughout this century they have worked hard to throw off all European models, and forge not just a new society, but literally a new way of life. And they are on the verge of doing exactly that.

Not for Gloria the structure of high birth, the distinction of military uniforms, ball gowns and jewels, or family names that speak of European titles. To say that you were impatient with all of that would be another understatement. You're one of those who came to throw over a last vestige of that heritage through the country and the continent of your birth. Is that clear to you?

Gloria: Yes.

Brian: You have nothing important left to learn from Freudian method. But you may have a great deal left to learn from contemporary Freudians. Continue to seek them out. Continue to hear them, men and women both. Continue to draw near and literally touch them with your hands.

You're in that stream. You're a part of it. Its essence is not in the books or the theory. It is no accident that you learned it from daughters of the church, a secret revolutionary society on the continent in which you grew up. Do you understand?

Gloria: Yes.

Brian: They had no links to the church which ordained them. Those sisters had no links to the masculine patrimony of professional Europe. They forged their own way, and they faced the forces that stirred in the souls of those who came to them for therapy, who honestly came for comfort and succor. Do you understand?

Gloria: I don't understand the last word. Succor?

Brian: Succor. Females give suck to infants; that is succor.

Gloria: Mm-hmm.

Brian: The sisters in that order gave the milk of human kindness to souls in their therapeutic work, far more by understanding and loving them than by giving them Freudian insights. Do you understand?

Gloria: Yes.

Brian: All right. You acquired that whole from them. You won't outgrow it and leave it behind. You'll continue to share it and grow with it. You carry that flame, that light, and that seed forward. You're a part of that company. Do you understand?

Gloria: Yes.

Brian: In that sense you too are a sister in that order. Do you understand?

Gloria: Yes.

Brian: The real order does not exist in some charter filed away in the Vatican. It lives in spirit, and it is spirit that shapes those women, their patients, the young, and the young born to those patients; you too. Your real commission, your real license to practice, rests in spirit. Your supervisors are in spirit, and you are measured by the rule of an order which has no house on earth. Do you understand?

Gloria: Yes.

Brian: Its house is in spirit. It animates you. It fills you with wisdom with every seeker who comes to your consultation room. It animates you when you undertake a creative project. The vibration of that soul family, of which you are a grown-up and functioning part, is what is ultimately conveyed in your films, your images, your creative acts. This is done just as great musicians convey a message which is almost never explicit in the lyrics, but instead is born in the *harmonies* above all. It's in the rhythms to a lesser extent. The sisterhood of which you are a part shines through everything you do.

As you face your patients' dark contents, the cruelty, the failures of parents, the blows and the indifferences of society as your patients have experienced them, you convey to them the strength, the courage, the *fearlessness* more properly, of the jungle animals. Confront a jaguar in the forest. He will snarl. He will choose whether to attack or run, but he will not know fear.

That's you when you enter the inner life of your patients. Do you understand? You do not know fear. You choose among your tools. You convey both strength and fearlessness in facing those contents. You also convey acceptance of their faults and deficiencies, but you do not cherish their weaknesses, their limitations, the attitudes that they have ingested which cripple them as functioning beings. You confront them. Do you understand?

Gloria: Yes.

Brian: That is your gift. You came to be this, and you are this. Yes, you travel now in North America, but you're not done with South America. Just as shamans once left the jungles of South America and traveled to North America, even to the Arctic reaches of North America; and yes, even to China, Southeast Asia, the Philippines, and the islands of the Pacific; and then brought home to their jungle people emblems, and goods, and often mothers and children, to mix into their own societies and help them find a place. And then went out again, and came back again, often for several lives in succession.

That is your pattern again this time. Do you understand? Those shamans were the sages of their societies. Their initiations were not about smoke, not about hallucinogens or visions. They transmitted what they transmitted through touch, just as you do. Do you understand?

Gloria: A little bit.

Brian: When patients come to you, you take their beings into your being. You change them, and you give it back to them. You have given birth to scenes which will unfold over 20, 30, 40, 50 years. It would not have found life if you had not touched it. Just wait for a minute while that sinks in.

You will of course continue to travel. You will of course continue to see patients. You will of course carry ideas back and forth from other continents home to your own continent. You are leading that continent into a whole new world, almost unglimpsed by its inhabitants. You are still a pioneer, and you are magnificently equipped to be that pioneer. It was that time in Vienna that made you so. Do you understand that?

Gloria: Yes.

Brian: All right. Do you need more Freudian training? No. Do you need to stay in touch with your colleagues, meet the best voices in this tradition? You surely do. You need to touch their hands. You need to listen to their voices. You need to sit in front of them eye-to-eye as an equal, and take in their beings, and they will cause new understandings to blossom in your being, even if you're not one bit interested in whatever concept they happen to be talking about. Do you understand that?

Gloria: Yes.

Brian: All right. Those forces that come out of the jungle are being reshaped with a new life on that South American continent. Those forces have nothing to learn about the beauty of the plant kingdom, about the joys of sex and conception, about the fearlessness of the hunt and combat. These things they have mastered for millions of years. They will change as they learn the values of what we call civilization, compassion, mercy, and above all, the spiritual dimensions of sex and conception. You understand these things; all three. You're shaping a continent still driven, for the most part, by those energies in their rawest form. Do you understand that?

Gloria: Yes.

Brian: All right. That's your task and your mission. You are perfectly prepared. The great events of your life, the same ones you've been taught to look at through a personal lens, were in truth carefully designed and served to you as training grounds, and we'll look at those through this larger lens as we move onto question two.

Gloria: I cannot think.

Brian: We can wait …

Gloria: Why did I choose a mother of steel? At times, I'll observe people who had great relationships with their mothers, and wonder how sweet it must be to have a loving mother. I didn't feel love from her towards me. Why did I have her as my mother in this life? Her name is Maria M———-, and she was born in Padua, Italy on December ------, 1933.

Brian: All right. We see a symbol, and we're going to unfold it. We see a silver helmet with a white plume. This plume is not an egret feather. It's the tail of a white horse. This plume is fastened to a helmet plated with sterling silver, having a carapace covering the neck, having a brief bill, having a round, tall dome over the head. It's a helmet that was worn in the 18th and 19th centuries by Hussars and other horse soldiers.

It's been a long time since these helmets were worn in combat, but they are worn to this day by those horsemen and horsewomen who train horses to dance while their horses receive orders through the heels of their riders as the riders sit erect and almost motionless in their saddles.

This is an ancient, ancient art. The great armies of Egypt and Babylon had men and women who did the same. Part showmanship, part horsemanship, part cavalry training, but in reality, encouraged and preserved by the Universal Forces, who say, "These horses, seen through universal eyes, are beings no less than you humans. You who have troubled to operate in concert with them until you are one soul and one mind hold an important secret for humankind." Horses have now been freed from warfare and that freedom is in accord with Universal Law. It was never lawful to send horses into war.

Your mother brought into her life a soul whose inner core was that kind of detail-oriented discipline. She had that kind of sky-high expectations for her offspring. Although it may not have found expression in the words she used, it did find expression in her perfectly straight back and in her perfectly fixed and unchanging requirements of you. Honestly, the way you experienced her will was as *heels dug into your sides.*

The pressure never eased. She had expectations of you. They were conveyed to you very, very consistently, and almost wordlessly. You could not be at ease with her. She was training you. That was her understanding of a mother's role. Do you understand that?

Gloria: Yes.

Brian: She wanted you "to perform honorably according to her expectations." Does that make sense to you?

Gloria: Yes, it does…

Brian: All right. Did she love you? *In her way.* Her way was possessive. Her way of love allowed no scope, no freedom for your independent development of values not conveyed by the family structure as she understood it. Does that make sense to you?

Gloria: Yes.

Brian: I think she would say, "I was a good mother. I did my job." Did she enjoy your company as you want to enjoy your daughter's company? *It never occurred to her.* Do you understand? To relish your innocence, your creativity, the flow of unpredictable, joyful life into hers, things which as a daughter you had to give. Does she have regrets about this? Honestly, no, Gloria. She does not yet see it. Is she disappointed in her own performance as a mother? Yes, privately. She thinks she should have been more disciplined. Do you understand?

Gloria: Yes.

Brian: Okay. She thinks she should have been more effective in turning you into her image. That's a regret she has. She does sometimes look on you with wonder at the person you've become. I'm not sure that comes out of her mouth. Do you understand that?

Gloria: Yes.

Brian: All right. There is a healing ahead. She will leave this body before long. She will review her life and values. Not to encourage regrets, that's not how those life reviews are structured. Not even to say, "Here you had an opportunity to give love, and receive it in return."

No. She'll be shown the values and ideas that she served, and she'll be shown the values, and ideas, and the love that was around her as the ocean is around a fish. She will recover the wholeness of her soul, the parts she didn't bring to this experience.

When that happens, you in your quiet times will experience the presence of her soul, Gloria. Her *soul*, not her personality. The presence of her soul restored to its wholeness, which is radiant, loving, accepting, and in her case, graceful. That was one of her prime soul characteristics. It found an unusual expression in this life and this existence. She does understand graceful beauty. Honestly, she learned it from the horses. She didn't really learn to see it in people in this existence. Do you understand that?

Gloria: Yes.

Brian: Her inner fund of grace did not find much expression in this life. In appearances? Yes. In a fine mind? Yes.

But oh, the kind of beautiful strength and acceptance that horses radiate, she did not express in this existence. She will recover it when she is restored to her soul. Look forward to that. She will visit you in that fuller expression of her reality. Do you understand?

Gloria: Yes.

Brian: Why did you choose such a mother? You chose to be a strong woman in this life. You chose *not* to be the kind of strong, disciplined, courageous intellectual that you were in that life as an analyst, and in several other lives.

You have been a commander in ancient Republican Rome. You have been a Consul in ancient Rome. You have been a philosopher more than once.

This time you said, "I'm going to be a woman. Motherhood, the love of a man, sex itself, I will experience as a woman, with the full cascading flow of a woman's emotions. Not with the fine analytical mind of a man who has mastered government and generalship."

The values that underlie European civilization, which of course are changing now; that generation that came born for the first World War; the first souls born during World War II, and those that have come since, are utterly transforming European life and heritage. They're transforming government too, although the full force has not yet been felt.

You came saying, "I'm coming into this new wave of world citizens as a woman. Not as a philosopher, not as a . . . politician's not the word; but not as a government leader, and not as a professor; *as a woman*."

You chose a woman for a mother whose grip on the kind of woman you meant to be was slender. She was not a woman who said, "I will know empathy." Not a woman who said, "I will know what it means to melt into the body of my infant and into the body of my lover." She didn't have those experiences.

She taught you discipline. She taught you to value your fine mind, but you had to find, for yourself, your deepest, strongest values as a woman. This was the challenge you undertook in selecting her as a mother. You had to discover it for yourself, because she did not model these values for you. You chose a hard walk. Do you understand?

Gloria: Yes.

Brian: You have succeeded. You did not become your mother's daughter. You became something quite original. You have become what you set out to become, and you are far from done. Do you understand?

Gloria: Good!

Brian: Yes. It's the forces coming out of spirit that will draw out of you the changes and the new expressions that will mark the rest of your life. It will not be your experiences as a young girl, not your childhood or infant experiences in the household of your parents. Every time you go within, whether it be in meditation, whether it be with a group of like-minded souls doing ayahuasca, whether it be in song, in music, in love; you strengthen, empower, and — we'll coin a word — *empassion* a new woman.

The roots of your childhood are withered and unimportant. Let's let that sink in for a minute. It's not a Freudian idea. Do you understand?

Gloria: I do.

Brian: All right. You will be reconciled with her. You will continue, as you already have, to love your daughter as your mother never loved you. She did love you in her way. It wasn't even a second-best way.

There are many ways for a soul to express love, and souls frequently take on very unpleasant assignments, seemingly as very limited people, in order to play a role in the unfoldment of their family, and of their children.

She has filled her role, and when she arrives on the other side and sees it whole, she'll feel satisfaction and some relief. And she won't ask for this kind of assignment again. Do you understand? She had her own lessons. She'll never again put on the helmet of the warrior. Do you understand?

Gloria: Yes.

Brian: All right. She may re-enter your family stream down the line as an infant. If she does, you'll be told, but nothing in the personality of that infant will reveal her past as your mother. She's done with it. She did it right to the hilt. Do you understand?

Gloria: Okay.

Brian: All right. There's love ahead, but you're under no obligation to feel tender love for the person you have known. Your acceptance of what she has been to you will come in time and come through your soul. Do you understand that?

Gloria: Yes.

Brian: All right. It has often happened in our time on earth that men have learned compassion in the most unlikely school. They've learned it in war by caring for their comrades, by missing them when they're killed, by tending them when they're wounded.

It's part of a process soon to bear fruit, as mankind puts away war as part of society. You and I may not see it, but the process is well underway. Paradoxical as it may seem, men are going to war far more conscious of what life can be than they've gone to war in the last several hundred years. That's just an aside.

All right. Your mother came to approach that lesson from a different standpoint. Her life was greatly affected by the situations in Italy in the nineteen thirties and forties. She was delivered from that. Those situations came powerfully into her life, and helped her shed at last the values of a disciplined military officer. She came to do that.

Gloria: Yes.

Brian: All right. You'll be reunited with your mother and it will be good. It'll be quite a while. Have I answered that question?

Gloria: Yes.

Brian: it was a setup, Gloria! You asked for it. You knew what you were getting into. It worked for you as it was designed to work, and you found in your own life streams of tenderness and compassion you could not have learned at her knee. She didn't teach you those expressions. You found them for yourself, and they don't resemble hers.

The remainder of Gloria's reading was devoted to the health of her grown children, something we often see with older mothers and even more often with grandmothers. The Record Keepers don't seem to mind, but they often show me the impression of the grown children on the seeker's own soul, not showing me the child's Record directly. I believe this is a consideration of privacy. And it sometimes happens that the grown child will "appear" in the reading room whether they are alive or dead to express their reservations about Mom knowing too much. I have seen this especially in the case of alcoholic or addicted children – they feel considerable shame about what they are making of this life's opportunity.

Given in the District of Columbia
October 2016

Jan Wakes Up to Fear and Dread

Chapter 9

JAN WAS REFERRED TO ME BY A DOCTOR who sometimes sends me a patient for a reading. Early in our relationship I said to that doctor that my readings were not for everybody, they really were meant for people who want to live out of their souls; and they are also for people to whom meditation is at the center of health. Those have been the doctor's guidelines ever since.

That's all I really knew about Jan when we met at a coffee shop.

There I learned that she was a consultant who helped resolve conflicts in nonprofit corporations, and the work took her all over the United States and Europe. It was a challenging and stressful life for a woman in her sixties.

Jan called me. She didn't tell me what the medical problem was and I didn't hear it from the doctor either. As we emailed back and forth, making our appointment, Jan wrote this to me:

"I'm not clear on what my questions are other than, one: What is meant to be the highest and best use of my life's remaining journey, that will bring me the greatest happiness and peace? Two: What is the seat or source of my anger? Three: What health conditions may I be facing, and how shall I treat them? Surprise! Now that I put them to paper they seem pretty clear."

I also learned that she renewed herself each summer on a Greek island in the Aegean Sea, where she lived on or near farms, and adapted her days to the rhythms of those farms. This she had done for years. Her face shone as she talked about these summers.

I also learned that she was a warm woman with a wonderful sense of gentle humor. I learned nothing about the state of her health, which I asked her not to disclose at this meeting. As I told her, knowing too much in advance of a reading only causes doubts to nag at the corners of my consciousness as I read. She also said that readings, prophecy, psychics, even scripture had never been important in her life.

When she arrived a few days later for the reading, she did not focus on health first. She did tell me in passing that the doctor was most concerned with the state of her bronchial passages, and she had been given medication to relieve those passages and address chest pain. But the element of urgency changed with her first question in the reading experience: "Why do I wake up these mornings with fear and dread?" The answer began,

> Brian: We see a symbol and it's a little silly. We'll have to unfold it. It's a banana ... this banana speaks of a former time. It's a former life, but these memories have been quite directly reawakened in this life. That former life was in what we might call Central America.
>
> We see an androgynous person. Not with the marked androgyny that we may see sometimes in young persons, but the kind of androgyny that comes to persons of advanced age who have realized their male and

female parts in expression for long years at a time. Such persons therefore become gentle, wise, and harmless, and at the same time, able to be bold and fearless in both speech and action.

This Central American existence was a former life lived as what we might call a high priest or a senior shaman or a sage. We don't really have a word for what you were in that time. You were that in a civilization that was, in its understandings of the soul, in its understandings of justice, in its understandings of how to relate to the earth, to agriculture, and to what we'll have to call "public health;" every bit as advanced as we are or think we are today.

This was a culture that has vanished and left almost no physical traces. Its technology was based on wood and stone and thatch. Such societies don't leave much for the archeologist to ponder. It was a sophisticated, urbanized, productive, and peaceful society that lasted several hundred years, a long time for a culture on this earth.

You were an honored person in that society. Above all, you were a person who lived without defenses, without mental defenses or habitual defenses, totally unacquainted with the weapons of war or even with the weapons of -- let's call it "political maneuvering." Your power came from the universal recognition of your wisdom. You did not need to defend yourself at any time in any way. So when conquest came out of the jungle into the city, you not only were surprised, you quite literally were unaware. Warriors came up the hill on which your dwelling was placed, a low hill, perhaps twenty feet high, with a dwelling mostly built of post and thatch.

They came, they threw you from your hammock, and killed you with shouts and curses. There lingers deep in your consciousness the memory of that truly horrific awakening, as violence burst over you, literally at the hour you customarily devoted to your prayers and meditations. On this day sunrise became the hour of curses and shouts and murder. That's why these feelings are associated with the hour of awakening.

In this life, at least at this point in your life, there is no one who wishes you physical harm, there are no forces which will come out of this jungle or any kind of jungle to slay you without warning. For that reason you don't have words for these fears. You're totally unconscious of such forces in this life.

Your way of working now is truly identical to the way of working which that sage had so long ago. He lived, incidentally, in that place which today we call Quintana Roo, the easternmost state in Mexico.

Jan, it hasn't been your habit in this life to pray to the sun as the sun rises. In that former life, you began each day literally attuning the energies of your body and your aura to the sun. You went through each day utterly believing that as you were giving to the people around you, you were expressing the gifts of the sun. You still do that, even though that language is not familiar to you in this time.

As a person, Jan, you are quite aware. You have entirely recaptured the ability to find peace, meaning, and rejuvenation surrounded by agriculture, domesticated animals, and the sounds that drift in from the fields. Truly that has been your natural habitat, far more than the cities and the civilization through which you have had to make your way.

So I was seeing here a woman who has drawn wonderfully on the understandings she made her own in a former life, but now had come upon what we might think of as a rock in the path, a kind of unmarked hazard that veered her into difficulties without preamble or warning. Jan hadn't been a person who focused on the unconscious mind or its workings but she grasped this right away.

In our talk at the coffee shop she had said, "I don't really know how to describe what I do, except that it works and people value it. Somehow, though, it sets me apart from most of the people I know, even in the world that values my work."

As the reading went on, the problem of waking in dread and its solution were not put in psychological or behavioral or even health terms:

Brian: Now, to end this pattern of dread: for twenty-one days, rise ten minutes before the sun comes up, seat yourself on a cushion in contact with earth or brick or stone, and praise the rising sun. Make a prayer. Our prayers are more powerful when spoken out loud. Pray that you will be energized and supported and made powerful, as surely as this earth is energized, supported, and made powerful by that rising sun. Wake up then knowing what you're going to do for the next fifteen minutes, and that other negative experience will vanish from your life.

Greet that sun as that spirit which lives within you, which is your uttermost and wisest friend, which heals your body and your emotions, which takes away your fatigue, which reduces all conflicts to the proper size. Every conflict can be handled by humans on earth, especially the conflicts between humans, and you know that very well.

At that point, in the midst of the reading, she was asked,

Brian: Can you do that? Will you do it?

Jan: Yes, I can do that. And I will do it.

Then she was told that pledges made in the reading situation are not only honored, but in keeping that pledge she would be reinforced "as only spirit can reinforce a body and build a good habit." That is, she made a contract to be met and helped, in a particular and almost concrete way, by spirit. On that note we moved to her second concern and its origin was given largely in physical terms. But in an additional note, Jan was given the soul patterns that have made this experience so different in kind for her.

Jan: I've been experiencing episodes of anger. Where does this come from?

Brian: Moving past the superficial facts of these incidents, we look at what in your body has gone awry and what in your body has diminished.

Well, it's the hormonal response that you have practiced all your life to quench anger before it flows freely. Of course that has its mental components as you've applied the things you know, and as with most of us, applied the slogans that we file these things under. But really, when we're challenged by surprise, or insulted, or suddenly find ourselves in danger -- it's not what we *think* so much as the hormonal pattern in the brain, in the emotions, and in the solar plexus, that arrests the spontaneous reaction, and lets you express instead what you have practiced and believed in. So where in this body have we lost that response?

We're seeing the lymph circulating in the brain. It's only been in recent years that medicine has recognized that the brain is richly supplied with lymph through its own channels, not so easily spotted, say, on autopsy. Lymph throughout our bodies is the immune system's first line of defense, and it causes inflammation when that is needed to quench an infection; lymph carries off dead cells when that is needed to heal from an injury or an insult; and lymph addresses those un-programmed cell growths we usually refer to as cancers.

Lymph in the body is central to all of these things. Lymph in the brain does all of these things too. Lymph will inflame the brain when there is damage to be healed, whether from a head injury, from a bleed, or from a minor stroke or the like.

But lymph also conducts healing properties – and endocrine substances too, in accordance with their physical and chemical properties. Plus it conducts the endocrines' energetic properties, just as the foods we take into our bodies have wavelengths and other healing properties.

These properties heal the brain. They heal the brain of anger, insults, even of resentments; honestly, even of questions that haunt us, say after a loss, a defeat, or a death. Brains need physical healing after these events.

We see the lymph circulation through the entire upper portion of your cranium, not neglecting the cerebrospinal fluid. We see inflammation there, so that the lymph in your head is literally having to heal those irritated conditions on the surface of the brain. To aid your body here, let's furnish the nutrients your endocrines need to aid this lymph.

What's being recommended here is that you start each day with a smoothie, and make that smoothie with some ice cubes, two or three ounces of almond milk, some fruit juice, fresh or canned; and apple juice, grape juice, white grape juice, and when you can get good, ripe ones, a few chunks of mango; or banana or any other fruit that looks good. And for the most important part: shell a couple of pecans, grind them in a coffee grinder, and add them to the smoothie. All together this will make five or six ounces of fluid. You should drink that.

Don't have anything else for breakfast in the next hour. The live factors in those pecans, aided by the live factors from the fruit and the juices, will provide your lymph manufactories with the factors needed to make the right balance in the lymph that's healing this condition in your brain, which is not however a disease condition. But this remedy does not address the cause of this inflammation.

Jan, you have a loss. That loss has diminished your confidence that you have a right to be here and be happy. You have lost a loved one, not so recently either. Three to five years ago is what I'm seeing here. This is a person older than you, and a person, like the sage you were, not so readily described by gender … a wise person too. Does this ring a bell for you?"

Jan: I need your help to see this.

Brian: What is your mother's condition?

Jan: She's in a wheelchair in assisted living. She's had increasing dementia. She lost my father about five years ago, and to her, that was the end of her life. She often says she doesn't want to be here anymore.

Then we reach back once more to a former life, to see and flesh out a soul pattern that truly has lit Jan's relationship with her mother all these years.

Brian: "I'm seeing a crown of thin but curly and really magnificent white hair. I see the name: Pat, or Patricia.

Jan: My mother's name is Pat – Patricia – but she's alive!

Brian: Yes, but largely withdrawn into spirit, though she still plays her part as a member of your soul family. Now her love and support for you flow to you on a different wavelength. You experience that as a loss. You miss her, and you have a rage about that. "Why? is the substance of that rage. Why is she not here beside me? Why can't I speak to her and enjoy her company, as I have for most of my life?"

Can you pray for her that she enjoy and grow and prosper in that new life she has already begun? All right. Make that prayer without guilt. Pray for her that her exit from this body will be just as smooth and untroubled as she hoped it would be when she chose this path out of this life. You're not called upon to hasten her exit or support her in any way differently than you're doing now. Know that she's totally at peace with what she's experiencing. That should be a comfort to you. Know that she's excited by the life her soul is now engaged upon. She can give to you as much or more as she ever gave.

See her now and know that she literally has another existence. She is a soul largely set free of earthly bonds and limitations. As her mind roams free in what you might think of as the pastures of unconnected memory, she's not suffering. Many people choose dementia as the way out of a life because in their lives they may have suffered, or had deaths that were a little too heroic to easily recover from. Dementia, for the person who has it, honestly is a pretty easy path. Do you understand that?

Jan: Mm-hmm ... yes.

Brian: Your mother is becoming a whole soul again. She'll always be your mother, but she's much more, and always was. I see that you have been her mother in other lives. The two of you have a total harmony on what being a mother means. You understood the choices she made as a mother. You understood the means she used to fashion a family. You would have liked to be beside her as her equal at the head of the family. Your siblings felt that too, and that was true from your earliest years.

Look back now to an island life when you were twin sisters. You made your lives in the same village. You married brothers, and you raised your children in what really was quite a large and closely bonded family. You were twin mothers as well, able to care for each other's children, able to love each other's spouses without friction or difficulties. It was a harmonious life, and sheep figured in this life. To this day you can't look at a sheep without feeling some affection and a personal connection. Isn't that true?

Jan: Yes!

Brian: Your mother accepted the life that you chose this time, a life path different from what she might have chosen for you, but she did accept it. She was able to accept it because of the deep love, but more than that, the deep, deep trust between you. It was the fundamental note of your relationship. Can you feel that?

Jan: Hmmm, yes.

The conductor asks, "Is there anything else that could or should be given at this time?"

Brian: Do you hear those birds, Jan? (Birds have begun to sing outside the window.)

Jan: Yes, I do.

Brian: They've been asked to be here. In the life we talked about in Central America, those birds were your -- honestly today we'd call them your "familiars." Do you know that phrase?

Jan: Somewhat.

Brian: Medieval Europeans claimed that every witch had a familiar animal who went out and did the witch's bidding. But that idea is the corruption of something very real. Every spiritual person has linked responses in the animal world, not among the domesticated animals, but among the wild ones. You are linked to birds, and not only in that life in Central America. That link was formed in a far more ancient life.

I'm going to test your credibility now. You were what we would call a physician on what are now the summits of the Cape Verde

Islands, off the Rock of Gibraltar in the Atlantic Ocean. Are you familiar with that? The Cape Verde Islands and the Canaries?

Jan: Yes, off Spain. Beyond Gibraltar? Out in the ocean?

Brian: Yes. A few hundred miles.

Jan: Out in the ocean. They have cows!

Brian: They do. Yes they do. Actually they have their own breed! It's unique in the world Those islands were formerly part of that infamous landmass known as Atlantis, not surrounded by the ocean in those days; and on the summits of those mountains were healing temples. You were a physician-priest in those temples. Those temples were thronged with doves. Do you know the sound that doves make?

Jan: Yes.

Brian: You worked all day, every day, to that sound. It was the musical soundtrack to the healing work you did. And you learned to hear in those lovely sounds the words that you needed to speak to the patients who came. Do you understand?

Jan: Mm-hmm. Yes, I do.

Brian: The doves spoke to you, you apprehended, and the words came out of your mouth. It was so natural to you, and you did it for so many years, that you were totally unconscious of what was happening. They were your companions. Ever since, birds have been your companions in every life. You've not always recognized them and loved them, but it's time in this life to renew that link. When you travel to a distant place, seek doves if you can find them, pigeons if you can't. Listen to those sounds. Be aware of them outside the windows of a meeting room. If you can, when you're staying someplace as you travel, find a place where the birds are numerous. They will absolutely convey peace to you, and as they did in that faraway life -- we are talking more than 100,000 years ago -- and they'll put into their music the words you're going to need in the days ahead.

That may stretch your understanding, but they literally do that. They're quite ready to do it again, quite ready to be intermediaries between those in spirit who guide you in your work and your body, your hearing, your organs of expression. I know I'm speaking on a high and poetic plane here. Do you understand?

Jan: I understand the doves, yes, I do.

Brian: Those dove sounds make peace in your being. This is only being given now because you need it. You're not as young as you used to be, and you feel the stress of your work more than you once did.

Jan: Mm-hmm, yes.

Brian: Now, something else. Whenever you can, whenever you take a vacation, however brief, take yourself to an island. As the deep ocean waves lap on the shore of an island, especially a small island, you hear their music and you apprehend their message. It's a timeless message. And if all human existence were wiped away by some unimaginable catastrophe tomorrow, those waves are telling you that everything that's important about the human stream would go on, as the old Atlanteans know. Do you understand?

Jan: Mm-hmm, yes.

Brian: Some people in Atlantis panicked and did bad things to their brothers and sisters as the end grew near. It didn't happen in a day. It happened over many generations. Other Atlanteans learned to tap the immortal, eternal parts of themselves and face the destruction of their civilization with equanimity and with good plans. You were among that group.

Consequently you are able to face the end of your life with equanimity and with good plans. And if you draw on the strengths these island – really, vibrations -- will give you, they will aid you to do that. Are you afraid of death?

Jan: In my quietest moments, no.

Brian: In your quietest moments … exactly what we need to build, more quiet moments.

You have it within you to face death as just another milestone, and that's all it is. But that's not what we believe as long as we fully occupy our bodies and our cultural experience. Let's build in that other resource that knows death to be a gateway to the next life, the life of the soul, which never ends and which is truly your life. As you seek this equanimity know that you're also preparing for that gateway whenever it comes. It's not imminent.

I've got to say one more thing: Your mother will be your tutor in these moments that you prepare for your own exit. She totally understands this gateway and this process. She's living out the one she chose, and she chose wisely for her soul. She'll help you prepare for your own. It'll feel quite familiar for that reason. That is a promise to you, and a blessing. With that, we'll be through for now.

Jan took this advice to heart and the terrible mornings ended shortly. Her episodes of anger faded from her experience and her equanimity returned.

She drew on other parts of the reading as she dealt with her mother's final illness, which worsened about a year after the reading. As Covid arrived in Florida, Jan brought her mother home from the nursing facility where she had been staying. Then she was a caregiver until her mother's passing eight months later. How she dealt with this stress is another story, but the insights given in this reading played a part.

Given in Florida
April, 2017
Conducted by Kathy Brackett

Christine

Chapter 9

ALTHOUGH SHE HAD RARELY HEARD OF AKASHIC READINGS or metaphysics either, Christine did become curious about readings I did while she visited with my family for a few weeks. She was an Austrian, 28, and she had studied Spanish at a language school in Colombia with my daughter. When she expressed an interest in the readings, I randomly chose a reading for her to sample. As it turned out, it was Aleisha's reading from Chapter 3. This was the reading about the young woman who lost her sister to a climbing accident, then was beaten badly without warning by her boyfriend.

I don't believe I could have chosen a more appropriate reading for her if I had known her for years. I had no idea what she might ask about, but she plunged right in with the concerns that were truly on her mind. The transcript begins after we ask the Record Keeper for her Book of Life:

Brian: I'm given this book by a white-haired man who's quite at home in the mountains that surround us. The book itself has a cover of ivory. Scattered throughout the surface of this cover are wildflower blossoms in lavender, purple, blue, yellow and pink, like a miniature meadow.

Taken together, these things tell us that the place of Christine's birth, the wavelengths of that earth and of the people who live there, are not coincidental. They were chosen to provide her with certain qualities, to fix them in her being for the rest of this life, for this is healthy ground. With that carefully chosen beginning in mind, let's proceed to the questions.

Susana, the conductor here: First question. Why were the deaths of Josef and Oliver so hard for me, that then I wasn't able to go to Julia's funeral?

Brian: These were contemporaries of yours, correct?

Christine: Mm-hmm, yes.

Brian: Was this an auto accident?

Christine: Yup, two of them. Together.

Brian: The violence of those accidents made an impact on your soul as if you had been in the car. Were you in the car?

Christine: No.

Brian: You may as well have been. You were wise not to go to Julia's funeral, wise to spare yourself as you recovered from this violence, which impacted your mind, your emotions, and even your body. And it took more than a year for you to restore the circulation of energy to normal patterns in your body after this loss.

When you think of new friends, and when you think of family, you do feel apprehension and fear that you could lose someone else. You've actually been afraid to grow close or even remain close to some older persons, because you don't want to lose them. You most especially do not want to experience the violent death of another as you did in these events.

We're going to come back to remedies to restore your confidence that life provides, restore your confidence that each of us is protected, that almost all deaths and illnesses, losses, and conflicts, are not fixed by fate exactly but do cast their shadows before them. And hard as it may be to understand, most of these appointments have been arranged and agreed to by your soul and by the souls of those involved. Honestly, Christine, they were on your schedule. That doesn't mean you caused them, or that you're in any way related, except as I just described. It's not a Christian idea. It's not an idea that we hold in the West, either, except among a very few.

We discussed this for some time, and Christine said that she had often thought of this, but had never really studied it. She said in so many words that loss was a concept, but in her feelings and in her daily life, the loss of energy and the strange sensations that she had never had before were not concepts. Why was it so heavy, why had it not improved in the two years since these accidents?

Brian: When joyful or tragic events occur, we literally have to re-organize and get used to the new way energy flows through our bodies. Do you understand that?

Christine: Yes.

Brian: You've had a blow, a blow no less severe than if you had been struck by a fist or a weapon. Those souls who passed from this earth also moved into a place and a plane of being that was prepared for them. I'm not being shown why this was so. I don't have their Records in front of me. I have only yours. Let's look at your Record in this regard.

Well, your soul has suffered from violet deaths. Of course, most souls have, but your soul suffered quite recently in this way. In World War Two, you were a soldier. First your comrades, and then you, lost your life violently in that war. But between the death of your comrades and your own death, you embraced a kind of fatalism. You said, "Of course I'm doomed, and this is what life is. This is what happens."

But that is not true. That's a conclusion that you drew, but drew in error. That's not what life is. Life is joyful, life is renewed.

Starting from there we discussed how souls prepare before a life. Life that exists before birth, and life that goes on after death -- these things had always been abstractions to Christine, ideas that were loosely and generally treated in church, but church had meant little to her.

The idea that we arrive in a life with some quite specific things to address and master: this was new to Christine. So was the idea that we plan our own lives, that something which endures from birth to death is truly a plan and a pattern that our souls create.

Brian: You came this time to face this lesson early, so you could find inside yourself the resources to love others, to pray for their happiness, to pray for their goals, their wishes and their loves. To pray with a light heart, even as the Angels do. So we'll talk about a remedy now. I want you to pray for Julia and for Oliver and for Josef. They have lives and their lives go on. If you loved each other, they're not absent from you ... they're not even absent from this room.

If little Luca or some other child delights you, think of these friends. They will instantly be there to share your delight. That is support -- you're sharing your life with them. Do you have a question about any of that? That is the natural way. That's how we interact with the ones we love and know in spirit.

We see now that your friends have embarked on new lives, planning, studying, and preparing. They will return stronger, renewed by their sojourn between lives. Your support matters to them. And because your love for them was real, their support matters to you. Do you have a question about that?

Christine: I don't know how to think about that.

Susana, the conductor here, reads Christine's second question: "Will I ever settle down and have my own kids and family? Shouldn't I be working on a career too?"

Brian: That's a big question … Christine, you're on that path. Your path isn't so conventional compared to what you learned growing up. You've not chosen a career, you've not chosen a mate for life, not chosen someone with whom to have these kids. But you will.

Your life plan is written in your Record, exactly as you made that plan, because *you* made it. You made it with help from the wisest friends and loves in your soul's experience.

In those planning sessions you said, "In my last life, I went heedlessly to war. I looked like a man, I died like a man, but I was a boy inside. I did not know how beautiful life is, what a miracle a child is."

We see that you planned this time not to have children until you have recovered the insights, the practice, and the rehearsals you took part in during your time between lives. So that you wouldn't enter marriage or motherhood as children do, planlessly. So that you will appreciate every step of that journey, so that you will heal the loss you experienced when you died as a soldier.

How should you be preparing at this time? Really, Christine, we see that in your plan the choice of career is secondary. The choice of someone to love and parent with is the most important choice you will ever make.

You wanted to make it as a grownup, and you can. You wanted to make it joyfully. You didn't want to make it accidentally. You truly didn't want to be influenced by alcohol or anything else that might cloud the flow of your soul's knowledge into the choices you make in this life.

Christine, that soldier dug quite a groove in your soul. That soldier made blunt the wounds of war through heavy alcohol use, as almost every soldier does. You know better in this life. But you are still vulnerable. There will be times when bad things happen and you'll feel the call of alcohol. It wants to be no part of choosing a husband and no part of conceiving a child. That's a very firm promise you made to yourself. Can you feel that?

Christine: Yeah.

Brian: Now, how can you heal more effectively at this time, in light of the gifts you carry in your soul? This is especially for you. In this world at this time, we don't understand color. There's nothing in this world, literally nothing -- not music, not sound, not even touch -- that heals as swiftly and as surely as the right colors taken in without fear.

The ancients knew that. In Atlantis, the people we would think of as doctors and nurses and therapists wore many, many colors, more than the rainbow. They filled their patients' dwelling places -- they weren't rooms exactly -- with every kind of color and they changed the patients' costumes frequently, because color in that time and place was an important part of therapeutic healing.

We've lost that. The Greeks knew it too, but it's been gone for several thousand years. They still know it in Asia, Christine. And they know that in Latin America too, and you know for yourself that they use color and love color in ways that just astonish us, don't they? It's not an accident that you've chosen to spend time there. Look forward to your return to South America. It's on your schedule too.

Soak up the colors, especially the colors the indigenous people wear. Enjoy the colors they paint their homes with, inside and out. Those colors are not foolish or accidental, they are an important part of their way of life. And they are important to you, more important than you have even dreamed.

The conductor reads Christine's written question three: "Would a career in social work fulfill me?"

Brian: If you see young men and women and children suffering because they cannot make it in society, you will suffer with them. You will feel their pain and you will feel that temptation to give up. I'm back to your soldier now, you see.

His uniform was not gray-green. His uniform was tan in color, trimmed in black. I'm not being shown which country he fought for. It was a European country.

He gave up on life. He saw too much, too much violence. He died because he let himself get careless. Do you understand? He died because he didn't hug the ground quickly enough when the artillery began. He died because he didn't conceal himself quickly enough, he died because he didn't cooperate as he needed to cooperate with the other soldiers in his squad. In that sense, his death was suicide.

Every time you plan for someone, you'll heal that soldier who died. He did not die foolishly, that's not the word. That soldier died to *escape*. Do you understand?

Christine: Yeah.

Brian: If you go into social work, you will meet people who escape by dodging their responsibilities, by drinking, by doing drugs, by running away, by never settling down, by finding one partner after another. That's whom you work with when you're in social work, and it would not be different if you were a teacher or a nurse. Do you understand?

Christine: Yeah.

Brian: Because nurses and teachers care for their clients too, in the same way that you would. You are a planner: you know that about yourself already. You will stretch and grow in your ability to love all kinds of people and in your ability to recover from the blows of life by planning for many. That's part of your own plan.

But this is more important: you will not marry to escape. Whatever you may need escaping from at that point in your life, you will not marry someone because he is strong. You will not marry someone who will keep you safe and protect you. You'll marry someone you want to enjoy things with. You'll marry someone you see as an equal, and you will want a man who sees you as an equal, not as a tender plant who needs to be protected.

Christine: Yes.

We discussed the time Christine spent planning with her soul family before she entered this incarnation. We saw a soul who wanted to be her child. And we saw three potential mates for her, three good choices really, whom she had gotten to know and admire during that "sojourn," the word we usually use for times between lives. We focused on one for whom the future would address something beyond the personal.

Brian: Susana, are we ready for the big question?

Conductor: Yes. Is there more that could or should be given at this time?

Brian: Well, I don't get to see this very often. I'm seeing a toddler. He's got your hair. He's got the sparkle you have in your eyes. When he's young, he'll have freckles. He watches you every day, even now. He's often with you when you're enjoying yourself. And you two will have a good relationship. And he says it's up to biology whether he will be the firstborn not. He'd like to be. Do you understand? He'd like to be in charge of those who will be his siblings.

So whether he comes first, second or third, it doesn't matter. He will be the strong one, the centerpiece, the one who brings joy to brothers or sisters and to you and to his father. That's part of his plan. And you and he have already practiced these things. You practiced your relationship in spirit before you came here.

The harmony will be extraordinary. That doesn't mean he'll be so easy to manage, okay? This is a lively boy, full of energy and healthy. That sparkle in his eye tells you that he's not going to be placid. Do you know that word?

Christine: Yes.

Brian: Peaceful like a perfectly still pond, that won't be him! He'll race from thing to thing. You'll enjoy it. He will stretch you a bit. You won't find it easy to say no to him. Of course, you must. Do you understand?

Christine: Yes.

Brian: All right. So that will be there as an area of growth when he arrives. And now I'm seeing some candidates for his father. There are more than one. Your mate is not destined. Do you understand?

Christine: Yes.

Brian: You have met several and evaluated each other in your time in preparation for this life. I see one warning: not a soldier. Do you understand?

Christine: Yes.

Brian: You would live in part the life a soldier lives if you marry one. Don't do it. You haven't prepared to do it. And the woman who marries a soldier should prepare before she comes to this earth. It's a hard walk.

Christine: Yes.

Brian: I'm looking at an engineer who does things that relate to water, as in building canals and locks and bridges. You could appreciate him. He's a planner too. He's a planner who is at peace with the earth and who enjoys responsibly shaping that earth and the flow of water, and responsibly providing for the community he lives in. That's one choice.

I'm seeing a musician. You made an impression on him. He didn't make such an impression on you. A man with light brown hair. But unlike some men, and unlike the impression you formed in your training group, your soul family, this is a responsible man. This is a man who could bring joy into your life through his associations with other music makers. Whether he's a musician himself or a manager or an administrator or even the operator of a theater, for this soul, music is the reason he's coming back. Do you understand?

Christine: Yes.

Brian: I see one more man. This is a man who wants to use science to heal. Not necessarily a doctor, probably not a doctor. But a soul who has prepared by learning the causes and the cures for the diseases your generation will have to meet.

We do that. We look ahead and we look for many. You probably know that in 1917, 1918, and 1919 many millions of people died from the flu. Do you know about this?

Christine: Yes.

Brian: They had prepared to do it, Christine. And the people who nursed them and who came up with remedies for them had prepared to do that too. And all of them, the victims, the patients, and the healers alike, had agreed to go through that. Because that ended World War I. Do you understand?

The world ran out of soldiers so fast that they ran out of people to work the factories and operate the cities too. They had to quit on that pointless war, so the end of the war wasn't about defeats and it wasn't about military victories. It was about too many flu deaths to go on.

This man has prepared. He's done the homework, studied that example. He has also studied an epidemic that will come to your generation too, one that will be first identified as a blood disease and then discovered to be not originating in blood. And you've prepared for that too. Your children will be immune. Do you understand?

Christine: Yes.

Brian: You have not looked for a person who would give you the genes you will need. Instead you have designed and prepared genes in your own body which will be transmitted to your children, so they will not be vulnerable to that epidemic. Remember that I don't know when it will occur or what it will be like. But you're not the first person I've seen that has prepared.

If this man is your choice for a mate, you will understand his choices for career and for contributing to and building strong communities. Do you understand?

Christine: Yes.

Brian: Three good paths, then. Were there others in your soul family? I don't see others. Are you destined to marry someone from your soul family? No. But it's always a good idea, and we'll leave that there. Christine, do you pray?

Christine: No.

Brian: Well, we need to change that. Make happy plans. Be clear, be thorough. Don't say, "Oh God, I want a car and I need it."

Say, "I was admiring a Volkswagen today. It was red, it had a green interior, it was new. I'd like one of those. I don't even have to deserve it, because I'm a good person and I belong in this world. So I don't know how you're going to do it, Lord, deliver that Volkswagen to me.

I won't be impatient but that's what I want. I'm a daughter of God. I deserve to have it. "

Brian: All right. With that, we will be through, and know that when you make such a prayer, the Angels rise up and they promise to deliver, the same way they deliver health, husbands and children. With that we will be through for now. All right, Susana.

Given in Florida, January 2020
Conducted by Susana Berry

Chris, Whose Father Died in the Viet Nam War

Chapter 10

FOR ALL OF HIS LIFE, CHRIS HAD BEEN A SINGER-SONGWRITER although he also made a career as an actor and as a performer in professional musical theater. He wanted a reading because he was troubled by mysteries that surrounded the death of his father, which occurred when Chris was only eighteen. He grieved, of course, but over time that grieving became something that lasted, and grew, and became central to his work and to what he was.

Dad was a pilot shot down in 1968, during the Viet Nam War. His plane went down in Laos, according to the report the family got. That report was very brief: "Killed in Action, Body Not Recovered." Chris's mom asked questions over the years, but very little emerged until the plane's wreckage was discovered in a jungle in 2005, thirty-seven years after it went down. Dad's shattered helmet was in the wreckage too, but there was no sign of his co-pilot's helmet. There were no remains of either man.

There were other jarring details too. The dogtags of Vincent, Dad's copilot, had turned up in another country, years after the war ended. There were other things that didn't fit, and at times the stories that came to the family from various military officials didn't match either. And there were complications: clearly the plane went down in Laos, where the United States was fighting an air war that was kept secret at the time and for five years afterward, so the evasions of official secrecy also undermined the family's trust in what they learned.

Of course for Chris the pain was personal. Dad was honored as a war hero at the time of his death and his fame lasted. So for Chris and his younger brother Tommy there was a legend to be lived up to, as they saw it. Tommy was fourteen when his dad died. Twenty years afterward, at thirty-four, Tommy took his own life. Once again mystery enveloped that death. Neither Chris nor his mother could accept the conclusions that were drawn about Tommy's death, which came as a surprise. Chris knew that Tommy was troubled at times but he had made a life and a career which appeared to be successful.

Brian: Chris's Book is gold, having a cover that is open in design, almost like fretwork. Beneath this lacy fretwork we see blue, sky blue. This is emblematic of a soul whose truth is only known when it's conveyed to another. This life was designed to do that and be that, to convey many kinds of truth and many kinds of vibrations, very little tinged with Chris's own opinion or experience. So his has been a performer's life. He has done this thing and continues to do it. With that kind of open transmission as a paramount characteristic of this incarnation let's proceed to the questions.

As his questions began, Chris asked, "What were the events of Dad's death, and what was the fate of Vincent?"

Brian speaks: first we see a slender, smiling, short-haired, distinguished-looking man. He's in a flight suit. He's relaxed. He wants you to know that yes, that plane went down on that mountain, and yes, he and Vincent were in the aircraft when it struck the ground. They did survive for a few hours. They were removed from the wreckage, not by soldiers, but by people whom we would describe as tribesmen. They were not sophisticated persons, not persons feeling they had some responsibility to a government or to any authority there. They removed these injured men, and both were still alive at that point. They simply hoped to be able to save their lives.

It was beyond what they could do. These men died a couple of thousand yards from the crash site. Their bodies were disposed of in the manner traditional to these people, lashed to platforms set high in the trees, and exposed to the elements.

This was done sincerely, with faith, not because they honored warriors so much, or Americans so much, but because that's what they would have done with one of their own had he died in a hunt or in combat. This was a people who rarely knew combat, but they had their traditions and they understood that much. These were not people who responded to the questions that were put to them, not at the time and not years later either. That's the fundamental reason for the shroud of mystery around these fliers' bodies and their fates.

Both men were conscious when they left the plane, yet they did not remain conscious long. Fundamentally, it was blood loss that took their lives. They had fractures, but they did not have internal injuries or head injuries, despite the shattered helmet. Vincent's helmet, in fact, was removed with him, intact. Vincent's dog tags were bartered by a people who understood very little about what dog tags were meant to accomplish, and they made their way through several changes of hands until they were acquired by people who gathered such things to sell in markets. These things would have included lighters, uniform items, weapons, anything that might bring a few coins in a country market.

They were prayed over. Your father wants you to know that. They were really blessed by those tribal people who removed them, and there were women among them, too. Truly it was a death more tender and not so sudden as the deaths that came to many of your father's colleagues and mates.

In the time that followed-- this is your father speaking to me now. he very soon recovered. To die in combat in this way was, of course, something he had thought of many times, and to the extent that anyone can, he had prepared himself to do it.

This is not news to you: duty was this man's life-spring. He did not feel that his duties ended with his death. Your father had been a warrior in more than one life. He understood that from the very start. Do you understand that?

Chris: Yes.

Brian: There was a period of recovery, not of re-education so much, but of learning to operate in the body of light in which he found himself, and then he returned to his duties, caring for those other pilots and crewmen who died as he died in that war. He moved on after a few years, about four years our time, to caring for those for whom recovery was a much longer process. They were those whose bodies were exploded by missiles or scattered in crashes, or who died before the guns of soldiers. They often did require periods of years, as we measure time, literally to reassemble their spiritual bodies, to sort out their perceptions, and to begin to function again … I'll put this simply: to function again as men, men who have passed into spirit, and who have tasks and study to undertake there.

It was clear to him that he had something to contribute, and equally clear to those who recovered him to spirit. He was a man of great responsibility, just as much on that other side as he was on this side.

Did your Dad draw near to his widow? To his sons? Yes, he did, from time to time, and then he delegated that task to family members better able to communicate, better able to comfort, honestly, better able to *mother* than he was.

Difficult as it was, Chris, that's when your education as a spiritual being began, not so much with words or visions. You became aware that there were many other sides, that Christian explanations were simply not adequate to the diversity and the love that you experienced and the love that came to you and your brother Tom. Almost all of this was done without words.

No coincidence then that you landed the role of Jesus. No coincidence then, and absolutely not a weakness, that you chose for the rest of your life to live with one foot in the other world and one foot in this one. Did you know that this would happen to you when you chose this incarnation? You knew it was likely, Chris. I'm going to pause for a moment to let that sink in. You knew it would be difficult. You also knew that with your art you could convey your understandings to those who needed to be lifted, needed to know that peace is not solely up to the warriors who fight to defend it, but to those great legions in spirit who comfort, lift up, who help make it possible for the survivors to go on. Do you understand that?

Chris: Yes I do.

Brian: Your father understood it. Your father did not see his job as limited to his own sons or his widow. He knew, he always knew, that as an Air Force officer he was part of something very large. He knew that those things he was equipped to do were where he should concentrate.

Did he love you? Deeply. And your brother, and your mother. Was there pain involved in making these choices? Yes. He had help to deal with that pain too. Chris, he has comforted many. He has done a great work. He has trained many younger men, we'll use that word, in that work as well, because his understanding of the warrior's role, and the warrior's risks, and the warrior's soul preparation, was deep and timeless.

Now he steps back for a moment because there are many here who witness and honor him for the job he has done since that death. He continues to be a leader, and I'm told this is the language to use: a servant of freedom and of those who in the best sense defend it.

Is there something you would like to ask while he's with us?

Chris: Will we ever meet again?

Brian: Yes. Oh, yes. He's there at times in your quiet moments. He's often there when you perform. He's often there with you and with your wife. He's tremendously proud of you, and probably more than any other person in your life, he understands the work you do. Your vibration speaks directly to those who have had the experience you've had, and it's received.

Let's look at your mother. She lived her life out, and she *lived* it. Did that loss heal? It healed as much as it ever heals for most widows. She loved your father and she undertook that life for the love of him. To be the wife of a warrior was a great task for her to undertake. She was not a soul prepared to be invulnerable in that role, but she *overcame*. She is whole now. They love each other as deeply as they ever did.

Conductor: Is there anything else here to help Chris resolve the pain and the loss of his father's death?

Brian: Two things, I'm told. Conveyed to me not by your father but by those witnesses.

First take your eyes off those who conveyed to you half-truths. They listened to government policy more than they listened to their own hearts. There are such men and women in every war. And those who were not kept full faith with, those who paid such a price, must get over that … I don't want to use the bitter word … have to get over that *propaganda* that every man is cared for, that every family is supported as fully as possible. Those things were not true in that war or in any other war. Your father understood that.

And one more thing you need to know. These men did not die in terror. They died fighting to control their aircraft. They died in command of themselves and their emotions. It's not like the movies, Chris. They did their job until the last instant. That's where their consciousness was.

Now I'm going to use some words here that you may never have thought of in this context. Your father's job with those who pass is to teach those who die *self-love.* This is true despite the way they usually died, with a sense of having failed.

They scatter their energies, their subtle bodies. After these explosive deaths those subtle bodies have to be reassembled piece by piece. It's not a task like building a puzzle. It's a task of *acceptance*, just as when we dream or enter meditation, we often don't recognize the parts of ourselves that we meet. They don't recognize the parts of themselves as they are reassembled and integrated. Do you understand that?

Chris: I believe so.

Brian: All right. This task is a complex specialty. It's been a specialty on the other side since mankind has been on this plane. It's only become more difficult. The introduction of high explosives, high-speed aircraft, and some of the weapons that utilize -- how can I put this? High wavelength energies -- all of these things have had to be mastered on the other side by those who literally have had to research. The arrival of atomic weapons vastly complicated that task.

I'm going to leave that there, but there are legions of souls who have made that their job, to restore wholeness to these spirits so that they can go on, and live, or reincarnate and travel on, as in each separate case they do.

When you pass on, Chris, you will discover the enormous role that music plays in that task. Just as when you change the vibrations in a room you quite literally make souls whole. They accept parts of themselves they would never accept or recognize without your help. Through the love you convey they sense your understanding of soul life and human nature. When you leave this life you'll go on doing that work.

Our conductor here asks Chris's prepared question: "What can I learn here that can help me resolve the pain and questioning brought about by the suicide of my brother, Tommy, who died around 1988? Are Dad, Mom, and Tommy together now, and are they okay?"

Brian: All right. Let's take a minute. We have a change of cast here, a different set of witnesses, although your father is still nearby … Chris, were there drugs involved in Tommy's death? Some of the witnesses here are led by those who specialize in such deaths.

Chris: Not that I know of. He was really troubled with … he was less than thirty-two when he died, and he was troubled with questions about Dad. Also, he felt like he couldn't live up to the image that Dad left as a war hero.

Brian: We see that. Chris, he was never meant to live up to it. That's not the myth we live by in this country, is it? He did not design a soul to make a warrior. He designed quite another kind of soul for this incarnation.

Initially, he was attended by those who attend to all suicides, who are gentle and tender, and despite the teachings of some churches, utterly free of judgment. Suicide is a hazard on this plane like any other hazard. The soul, itself, however, may encounter quite a mass of guilt when it realizes that suicide has been the means of exit, and Tommy did. More or less, that made concrete his feeling that he could not be a hero, that he had somehow been a coward.

He was not a coward. He had prepared himself for another kind of life. He was quite sensitive. He was quite vulnerable. He kept to himself, honestly, Chris, the soul of a poet. He had things to say. He had things to write. He meant to be a poet. He had chosen for himself a gift that would have matured, had it been allowed to mature, in his late twenties. So he experienced the pain of having missed his calling, but he had no idea what that calling was. Do you understand?

Chris: Yes. He was very talented. He was an award-winning photographer and an up-and-coming architect.

Brian: Really, for Tommy, the burden was, "could he give what he had to give in a world where there was so much generalized violence?" That's how Tommy's soul perceived what made him struggle on this earth. It was beauty that he saw and beauty that he responded to. Beauty was the wavelength on which his own spiritual support was furnished to him. That beauty had nothing to do with the violence in the world that he saw around him, or the violence that he inevitably tuned in to after your father's death. You do remember that our society at that time was steeped in images of front-line war. The first society in history, ever, to have those images sent fresh into their living rooms. It created wounds and damage of a kind that were unprecedented.

Tom was a man very alive to images, their content, their nature. It took quite a toll on him. Not uniquely, for many another sensitive soul couldn't take that, and many another American, for the same reason, couldn't take it. That toll has never been added up, to this channel's knowledge, but it was real.

Now, has he recovered? Well, I'm seeing him at a drawing table. At this point in his soul's existence, he channels design, architecture, and typography to kindred souls who are in incarnation at this time. He has realized, oh we would say, the messages and the dreams that he brought with him into his own incarnation. He's passed them on to those kindred souls who have followed similar paths. He's at peace. He never would have elected a path that led him through fields of violence. Do you understand that? We'll use the big word: he's happy to be a soul who feeds other souls through Art.

In his sojourn on the inner planes he has realized the soul purposes of his incarnation as your brother. That's a very good message to be able to report, Chris. Some souls take quite a long time to recover from a suicide. In his case, as we measure time, he was a functioning and contributing soul again within about eight years, our time. You know, they don't really have time where he is. I'm trying to express that he did recover well and happily, and he is a happy soul now.

Will you see him when you pass? Yes, he'll be there for that reunion, and the love between you two will be undiminished, and will figure in your planning for your own future as a soul. Gosh, there's a great volume here. I'm not sure we can convey that now, and it's premature, but do you understand? The love between you two is a rich soul love, and it's not that you were twin souls exactly, but you were as close as two souls can be.

Conductor: Chris has worked for years on a film about the missing and others whose fates were hard to learn even after the war ended. The film's working title is "Not Forgotten." He has devoted many tours and benefit concerts to this cause and to raising money to complete the film. His research showed that there were more than 16,000 such cases. He wanted to understand things that would help him portray, accept, and find honest meaning in those deaths.

Chris: Is there anything specific that my father, my brother, my mother want to communicate to me, or our children, or to their great-grandchildren?

Brian: All right. The first answer comes directly from your father. He would like it if you could convey through your work that souls prepare to play the role that he played. While governments may prove inadequate, or even tumble, such souls as he are met with honor when they fall. They are supported with honor when they survive and go on to make other kinds of lives. He would like it very much if you could convey that message. He died a warrior with honor. He's proud to be that. He has no regrets about that aspect of his life. Do you understand?

Chris: I think so.

Brian: All right. You and I, and our generation, have walked a path where at times we may have had difficulty apprehending that there are warriors who live with honor. That's a complex picture. That's been part of the conflict that has lived within you.

Was his death in some sense necessary? Was his death a contribution to freedom for that nation or for this nation? The answer, Chris, is *yes*, through ways and means and channels far, far too complex to describe in a reading of this kind.

The role of the warrior has its place on earth. It's a difficult calling. Not all who die in uniform are truly warriors. It's a soul calling.

It's as a soul that people like your father prepare. The military training, the context, the lessons of history, the things he passed through as a young man mattered far less to him, even then, than did the training he underwent as a soul. And those things, the political conflicts, the human conflicts, more importantly, the troubles we have all had at recovering from that period, troubled him very little. He did his job and he understood his job and he's done it ever since. Do you understand that?

Chris: Yes, I think I do. And thank you.

Brian: One more thing. Yes. Yes, they want to communicate something very specific. They want to communicate to you, all of them, that their optimism, their hope, and their belief in what we set out to do in this country shines forth, undiminished

There is another part to this, and it will be conveyed in your film, through images, not through spoken words. That is that this earth in Indo-China was badly punished. It's not an accident that it was this earth that received your father and many another who fell. As you heal the survivors, and give comfort to the survivors of the war since, you'll also open our people to love that earth. Do you understand? That earth, Indo-China, is teeming with non-governmental organizations. Young people are there, not just from America, but from every Western country. They're healing that earth. They're healing that people.

Your film will show the beauty of that land, in its own terms. It doesn't have to be spelled out in language. That will be healing, too. A death in the jungle is as much a thing of beauty as every other kind of death. The jungle is kind to death. It receives those bodies and nourishes those spirits in ways so natural, so ancient, and so timeless.

Some of the images in your film will convey that to an American public that has no idea. Do you understand?

Chris: Yes, I do.

Brian: What else can be given? One very important thing. If you open in prayer to the values he lived, not just the courage, but the unselfishness that such warriors as he lived, peace will come to your soul.

He'll be there with you in the moment that peace comes. It is within reach for you, in this life, in this body, in this personality. You have the understanding, the meditative means, and the breadth of vision to apprehend the wisdom of your father's soul. Do you understand?

Chris: I do.

Brian: All right. You won't truly understand it until it occurs, when it settles over you as peace and acceptance and pride, all three things. With that promise, we will be through for now.

To begin reassembling a body of light by learning self-love: we read about that in Chapter 3, with Aleisha's sister Margaret. In this book we have dealt very little with dreams, but the need to recognize the unexpressed parts of ourselves is one of the most important parts of dream work. And that part of knowing ourselves is important to soul work, not just to specialists.

It counts every day as we face the things that come in dreams, which are really the reports of your soul about how that entity sees our own motives and actions, each day. Every dream then is a psychic reading delivered in bite-sized chunks, whose meaning is not difficult to discern once we realize how surely the dream is related to the actions and impressions of the preceding day. When we can face our dreams unafraid we are well along the road to wholeness.

To reassemble a body of light when death comes abruptly ... this too is a critical piece to coping with near death and after-death impressions and communications.

Given in Florida July, 2016
Conducted by Betty Labbate
Chris was on the telephone

Ruth and Radiation

Chapter 11

RUTH CALLED FOR A READING BECAUSE SHE WAS AFRAID. Four separate times she had been treated for Osteosarcoma, a cancer usually thought of as bone cancer, and she didn't know if it would return yet again. When we did the reading Ruth was 27. She was a Registered Nurse who worked in an intensive care unit. Other nurses in the medical center where she worked in her Midwestern state had offered her my name.

At the time she called she was still recovering from surgery on the parietal lobes of her cranium. These were all the facts I knew when we commenced the reading, yet there was so much confidence and vitality in her voice when she called, that truly I borrowed a little from her to push away my own doubts. You will read that courage of hers in her responses. Ruth's reading was done over the phone.

She wrote this to me the day she called: "It sounds crazy but I am completely healthy besides having cancer four times! My genetic testing results were normal so I used to think I was doing everything right. I feel like I was a random victim to this disease. I eat ridiculously healthy, sleep well, work out, do things I love, and I am surrounded by people that make me happy. After watching the documentary "Heal" on Netflix, I realized the importance of a healthy mind and the mind-body connection. That was like the missing piece. I decided that I would start meditating and I have felt a huge shift. This was also why I started seeing M-----, a therapist, and found you.

I am looking for more insight as to why my body can't keep these diseases at bay. I want to be healthy!" Her reading transcript begins:

Brian: We have this body and this Record, and it is unusual. I've never seen another book like it. It looks like the phone books we used to have forty and fifty years ago: thick, with hundreds of pages, and filled with tiny type. This is an old soul with a great many connections to other souls, to other times, and to sojourns between lives. Ruth has an enormous amount of support in spirit. With that in mind, let us proceed to the questions, Betty.

Betty, the conductor here: What is the current state of Ruth's body? What is the true state of these osteosarcomas, the sequelae of the surgeries, the cranial tumor, and any other tumorous conditions, recognized or unrecognized?

Brian: We do start with the head, and look at the cranium, both sides, parietal lobes of the brain as well. And we see a surgery that is not entirely healed but is healing well. We're seeing a picture that's pretty much ideal in the light of this recent history.

As the scan continued, we saw some unique arrangements in her organs and glands that had to do with healing from these illnesses and procedures. We saw evidence of radiation, a liver 25% larger than normal but functioning well despite a burden of inactive tissue, and lungs that were enlarged too, lungs whose capacity had simply expanded through all these episodes. We saw that these were not disease conditions but part of the body's own unique recovery plan. The same was said of Ruth's kidneys, which were also enlarged.

Brian: Now we are looking at the reproductive organs. Was yours a complete hysterectomy?

Ruth: I still have my ovaries.

Brian: All right, and the uterus is gone, is that correct?

Ruth: Correct.

Brian: Okay. It's not so easy to tell, because I scan the etheric body, and when we have surgeries, or when we have amputations, the etheric body retains the limb or body parts which have been removed. Does that sound familiar to you?

Ruth: No, I did not know that.

Brian: Okay, well if you look up phantom pain in the case of amputations, you'll see the story there.

Ruth: Oh yeah, I know all about phantom pain.

Brian: I can see why you might. You have an etheric body that's in recovery from these surgeries, and recovery from hysterectomy is a matter not of months, but honestly of years. You're still in that process. I am going to take a look at the rest of your skeleton in a minute, but now I'm going to look at that leg.

It's the right tibia that was operated on and reinforced with a metal plate, is that correct?

Ruth: Yes.

Brian: All right. That's been a long time, and those arrangements are happy and working for you. Let's go back up the spine and check on the rest of this skeleton. We are concerned about why the osteosarcoma has come back. We're going to have a question about that a little later, but I'm looking at your bones … looking now at the pelvis. I don't know how to describe what I see. There are ridged and raised surfaces on the inner surfaces of the pelvis. They do not suggest a tumor. They do suggest, really, osteosarcomas that have appeared and been healed, and apparently never reported. Is that correct?

Ruth: I don't know.

Brian: Well that's what I see. Is your left leg a little bit longer than your right?

Ruth: Yes, it is actually.

Brian: So the left ball and socket joint has been absorbing some of the blows that occur in that situation. There's nothing abnormal about that. I'm looking to see if this is something that reflects the work that was done on the tibia, because we don't always wind up with bones the same length when metal plates are put in … apparently not, is that answer.

Looking at the knees now. Looking at the tibia, the fibula, the femur in both legs, the kneecaps too. Your knees have made some adjustments over time, so you walk with an unusual gait. Might not be apparent to anyone, might not even be apparent to you, but you have made some adjustments in your gait. On the whole, these are not damaging adjustments. Can you run happily?

Ruth: No.

Brian: No. Where does pain occur?

Ruth: It's not a pain, it's more of a poor coordination thing with my leg.

Brian: Right leg?

Ruth: Yes.

Brian: Okay, let's look closely at that . . . well no surprise here, you do have some unusual muscular arrangements in that leg, and they're not ideal. But they're not a disease condition. And you have learned how to move to not exacerbate that condition. But you will honestly want to watch your gait for the rest of your life, and occasionally ask a physical therapist to evaluate your gait, do you understand?

Ruth: Mm-hmm. Yes.

Brian: All right, is there anything … I'm going to ask my physicians now, is there anything I have overlooked in the scan of this body? And they are checking … and they are reporting something at the base of the lungs: a little congestion, a little inflammation, even some irritation. And they say this is a lingering side effect of chemotherapy, because some chemo is eliminated through the lungs, and that appears to have happened to you. And it almost doesn't matter which chemo. Did you have chemo as part of the process for the hysterectomy?

Ruth: Yes.

Brian: That's the most likely culprit, they say. Let's move on from the scan and go to question two.

Conductor: Ruth has begun to meditate, sees a holistic counselor, and has maintained healthy habits of eating and exercise. What does she most need to know to manifest good health and prevent further disease? And is there some underlying global cause that makes her especially vulnerable to cancers?

Brian: Okay. A superficial review of your diet confirms that yes, it's wiser than most. We're not going to spend a lot of time on diet unless we get some very specific recommendations.

Let's look first at this: what in your body, what in your soul history has made you vulnerable to these cancers?

Now we find ourselves looking at the Akashic Record, which is the record of your soul, and does include any extraordinary physical conditions you've experienced in former lives as well. I'm being asked to look at your exposure to radiation. Not therapeutic radiation, but radiation as it is employed in medical centers and military settings. Do you have a work history in either of those places?

Ruth: No.

Brian: Okay. What is your occupation, Ruth?

Ruth: I'm a nurse. An ICU nurse.

Brian: An RN?

Ruth: Yes.

Brian: Now let's look at the Soul Path. What did you come back into this life to heal? I think that might give us some more answers.

Conductor: That's what I'm getting too.

Brian: All right, you have been a physician many times. In most of those lives, your attitudes and your approach to medicine were healthy. I'm reluctant to report what I see next, but I don't have a choice about that. You do have a recent life when you were a physician in the 1940's and the 1950's, and it occasionally fell to you to make determinations of risk in the exposure of military personnel to atomic weapons. Does that need to be explained to you, that troops, and sometimes sailors, were distributed around areas where atomic tests were conducted, literally as living guinea pigs? Are you familiar with that history in the 1950's?

Ruth: Yes.

Brian: All right. Well, no medical person's knowledge was adequate to make those determinations in those years, but your attitude was not ideal. I wouldn't say it was casual, but you tended to accept the data that were furnished to you, and you tended to make rather cursory examinations of the personnel exposed in those tests. Do you understand?

Ruth: Mm-hmm. Yes.

Brian: You have some deep misgivings about that in your soul. Let's look at that, and let's talk to --- I'm going to call them your "soul advisors," those entities and souls that have been with you in your many lives.

I'm seeing one silver-haired physician now whom you did actually knew in that time. His name was Armstrong, and he was a mentor to you. You were a young Army doctor, and as was so often the case in those years, your medical education was paid for by the Army. You trusted this man, and he rewarded your trust by being totally trustworthy as a mentor to you.

He wants you to know that despite the things that you have seen from what we call the "interbetween," your life between lives, you did as well as any other physician in examining and protecting the men who were given to you. He wants you to know you are not responsible for the various epidemics of cancers, particularly in the western states of North America, that have come about as a consequence of those tests. Osteosarcoma is among them. Do you understand?

Ruth: Yeah.

Brian: All right. He's going to explain this in simple and not medical language. Your soul has developed osteosarcomas in sympathy with those children -- and they are numerous -- in Nevada, Idaho, Utah, Missouri, and Arizona, who have suffered from osteosarcoma as a result of the atomic tests and the fallout in those areas. Do you have a question about what I just said? It's not a concept you may have encountered.

Ruth: No, I understand.

Brian: We all feel sympathy for children who develop cancer, and especially those who carry that cancer into their adult lives, and even into advanced age, as many, many have; scores of thousands in those states. For political reasons that data has never been collected.

I'm being shown a book that I have seen before. It's called *American Ground Zero.* It was written not by a medical person but by a photographer named Gallagher who toured those states in the 1990's and photographed some of those victims. You might take a look at that book.

But when you do, pray for those people without guilt. Pray for them, honestly, without pity. Prayers in which we extend pity don't help people. Pray for them that their lives be blessed, that their children and their grandchildren be free of this damage, which *is* recorded in the genes. Pray for them for their adjustment, that what was done to them will lead to good commitments and good interests in the lives that they're making now, and the lives that they will go on to make.

A great many of these souls have studied radiation and its link to illnesses, and many of these souls will be coming back as physicians and nurses and research scientists equipped to heal and reverse these damages. Do you understand?

Ruth: Yes.

Brian: Pray for them.

Conductor: Can I add?

Brian: Betty, do add.

Betty, the conductor: Ruth, what I'm getting is that your soul chose this journey because of your bad feelings about what you saw in that last lifetime, and so that's kind of why you've ended up with all these different osteosarcomas, et cetera. And what Brian is reading also is how to look at that, and to pray for them, et cetera, but also add yourself to that, so that you can release any feelings of sympathy and sadness. It was something that you saw, and in that last lifetime what I get is that you actually also died of cancer there, from absorbing it, from being in the same area and working with those patients, et cetera. And you came back to make that right.

So you came back to try to find a cure for this, and to try to work with patients again in that kind of area, so what I'm hearing is that you need to recognize it as what it is. But it is a past life piece, and you need to be in the present now. You can release yourself from any guilt, and release from any negative feelings around that. We've all had lifetimes when maybe we didn't do everything we were supposed to do. But that's what you came back here in this lifetime to do, from what I'm reading. This was the way you, or your soul, choose to go through it. I know Brian's going to give you some more information on how to work with that too, but that's what I'm getting also. This is a soul pattern that you chose to come in with, and I think your ultimate goal was to find an answer for how to heal the osteosarcomas.

Ruth: Oh. Umh hum, yes.

Brian: All right, Ruth, Betty is an RN too. You are a young nurse, young in your career. There's a lifetime stretching ahead of you, and this direction should not become an obsession or a fixation at all. Your ears have been opened. Your guides are aware of this, and have been, and you can live a balanced life as you pursue this knowledge. It's knowledge we're talking about. Are you married, Ruth?

Ruth: I am.

Brian: Is your husband in the medical field?

Ruth: He is studying to get into the medical field, yes.

Brian: Then I think you're going to find understanding and support as you develop a research interest in this field. The important part of what Betty said is, we live in the present. Guilt has no place for any of us in the present once we've gotten a message, and it has no place in your present either. Can you accept that?

Ruth: Yes.

Brian: All right. What you're healing from is horror felt in another life. It's no different for war veterans, it's no different for victims of the current wars, it's no different for the civilians in those areas who now are experiencing horrors, and will have their recoveries to make as they finish out these lives.

As they enter their sojourns between lives, and probably as they enter new lives as well, these -- I don't want to call them soul wounds, that's too dramatic a phrase -- these "shadows in soul memories and experiences" want to be dealt with in a healthy fashion. You said yourself you're a remarkably healthy person, cancers aside, and looking at your body, you really are. You're a capable person as well, this is written all through your being. I do think that this knowledge, cheerily ---literally cheerily -- applied in a balanced way, will see an end to sarcomas in your experience. Do you understand?

Ruth: Yeah.

Brian: All right. So, you're a meditator.

Ruth: Mm-hmm, yes.

Brian: This task, this interest, I'd rather call it an interest than a task; I don't want to call it karma. This interest will expand and grow, and you will find yourself hearing, seeing, encountering others on this same path. You will recognize each other. This will grow in a healthy way. I know it's been a rocky beginning, but I'm going to put this as it's given. This will become a joy to you. Do you understand?

Ruth: Yeah.

Brian: All right. Do we have a third question before we get to the final question we always use?

Conductor: No, that was pretty much it. She wanted the underlying global cause that made her vulnerable, and how she could manifest good health.

Brian: All right. It would do you no harm to discuss former lives with your counselor and any others she may recommend. She understands them. And karma's a big, big subject, all right? People spend lives understanding how it actually works out, but all karma is loving in its design. I said that, all right! Don't see this thing as a shadow that's tailing you and is going to bring you more grief. It is not. It's been a rough beginning, but it was only a beginning. I don't see more sarcomas in your future. And I'm not getting any corrections from our physicians on this case.

Doctor Armstrong you will meet face-to-face in your meditations in time. You'll recognize that wise voice. You will recognize ... how can I say this? ... the wisdom of an old soul who loves yours, who has perceived your life and your training and your practice as a nurse so far in this life. Do you understand?

Ruth: Yes.

Brian: I never say focus on a guide. I always say, focus on your own informed decisions that designed this life, its challenges and its gifts, because that is the source of your being. It's not the you that you're used to thinking about, but it's the you that you really are. Do you understand what I just said?

Ruth: Yes.

Brian: All right. That is your identity and the Source of your Being. When you pray, pray to draw closer to that. When guides appear, you already have protection; you can trust what comes.

Brian: All right. You're sounding quiet. Have I upset you?

Ruth: No, I'm just listening.

Brian: Okay. Well it's only going to get more interesting, and more compelling, as you uncover and live out what you find inside yourself. What kind of meditation are you doing?

Ruth: I listen to Joe Dizpenza CDs, they're 45 minutes long or so. They're like a guided meditation, and at the end there's probably like 20 minutes where it's just music.

Brian: Honestly that sounds ideal. Go on as you are, and in time you'll go on to other things. We all do. But you're in a good place. When you think about these cancers, are you afraid?

Ruth: Yes.

Brian: Good for you. That's a true response. Of course you are. We all would be. That fear will dissolve one day at a time as you apply the things you know, the habits you've built, the things that your helpers here on earth will help you with; and the things you've heard in this reading and what you will hear in your meditations.

Ruth: Actually the number one thing I'm working on with my counselor on is getting past fear.

Brian: Now we have a few minutes left, and we're going to ask the question we always ask at this point. Ready?

Conductor: Is there anything else that could or should be given at this time?

Brian: I see a symbol, I'm going to have to unfold it. I see a squirrel, and that's no more silly than most of the symbols that I see! And what is that squirrel doing? Squirreling away nuts for the winter. Squirreling away acorns that will grow into mighty oaks. Do you understand what I just said?

Ruth: Mm-hmm (affirmative).

Brian: Listen to this reading again about once a week, until you don't get any more surprises, do you understand? And those things that you're not hearing now, some of which are being given to you not in words, you will hear. And they will grow the way that squirrel's acorns grow, and they will make you strong and fearless, and you'll walk forward standing straight.

I know that's a poor little poem. The best I can do! All right, you are not alone. You strike me as a person of good humor, able to enjoy and learn from the people around you, able to recognize good values in another human being when you see them. Is that true?

Ruth: Yeah.

Brian: All right. Keep your eyes and ears open. You will not make this journey alone. Dr. Armstrong will make himself known to you before very long. That's a blessing and a promise. And you are on a good path. That's a blessing and a promise too. And with that, we will be through for now.

Given in Florida, November 2019
Conducted by Betty Labbate
Ruth was on the telephone

Gabriela, a Healer and a New Mother

Chapter12

GABRIELA WAS BORN IN FLORIDA to parents who started from Puerto Rico. Her family's life was clouded by violence and hardship, and she set out early on an independent existence. In time she studied massage therapy, and soon realized that she was doing healing. She became a healer even as she became a new parent. Caring for infants and new mothers became her passion, and Yoga, bodywork, nutrition, and child care were fields she felt called to master. She came for a reading wanting clarity about aligning these things with her life purpose.

Truly she came in the midst of her life, not with a lifetime behind her. The challenges she was living were the challenges of her generation and her cohort in Texas, where she made her home. She was a seeker who wanted insight, not a whole new direction.

She made an impression as an outwardly confident woman, outspoken and strong, with a voice and a body that only reinforced that picture. Despite this seeming clarity her reading held some surprises for her. The text of the reading begins here:

We have this Record, bound and covered today in ivory, carved in rounded shapes showing the forms of trees, bushes, and animals. These are small animals who might be encountered in a forest on a

Caribbean island. This cover speaks of a life planned with knowledge of the earth and its needs uppermost in mind, with a relationship to life, to birth, and to healing, as straightforward and fully supported by spirit as is the life of such animals in the forest. This will become clearer as we go along. Let's proceed to the questions.

Gabriela's first question was big: "What is my life path, my goal, my mission? How can I align with it effectively? Practically, what can I do to create the healing practice I want to have? I want to influence collective consciousness and our planet too."

Brian: We see a symbol first, and it's surprising. Let's unfold it. We see a quill pen, such as might have been used in the 18th or early in the 19th century, for this is a soul who has come to write what she learns and share it widely. This is a soul with a deep appreciation for the lasting power of the written word.

But in this lifetime, Gabriela, you have had difficulties writing what was expected of you. Often what came as you took a pen or keyboard in hand was the truth of what you saw, rather than the ideas and the words someone expected. Gabriela, you have a role and a mission to fulfill as a writer. In part as a recorder of what passes around you, what your friends and associates see, but also of your own ideas as well.

What else do we see here? We see a mortar and pestle, of simple earthenware, fired and glazed. For this soul has forged a relationship to the truths of herbal healing, built over at least three lives. This time meant to be expressed as a dedication to healthy food, especially healthy vegetables, healthy fruit, healthy soil and healthy methods of agriculture. To be conveyed not from a university pulpit, nor from a government agency post, but directly to those families for whom this will be a primary reason to gather together, to join their lives in loose and informal community, and raise their children. They mean to so raise them that they are attuned both to their parents' generation and to their own generation and to their purposes for entering the earth at this time. Gabriela, this is a planetary obligation. You have come in part to raise planetary consciousness about these issues.

We see something else now … we see an image of a large white bird, an egret, beautiful, of course. The beauty of the egret, plumed and elegant, is unique on the planet. Oh, what is this quality … a serene flier, not at great heights, but just above the earth, so that every eye turns to see and admire the beauty of a passing egret.

This symbol unfolds on several levels. You as a person are a message. Your writings and your example will be perceived by those who see you in passing. Your beauty, all of your beauty -- your physical beauty, your spiritual beauty, your beauty as a person acting fully in the communities and the society of your time -- will be like that of the egret, clearly rare to everyone who sees you, but also a little bit endangered.

Gabriela, in the first part of the last century egrets were all but erased from the earth by a fad for egret feathers in ladies' hats. But the egrets survived, and you will too. Simply be aware that your mission and your being are both unique but you are vulnerable in some important ways.

The egret is a shore bird, found everywhere in the Caribbean and around the Gulf of Mexico. That same subtropical vibration forms the fundamental note of your being in this lifetime.

We note in passing: this region will be the most changeful, the most fully supported from spirit, honestly the important region on earth, in the first half of your lifetime. That is the Caribbean, that Gulf of Mexico basin, and the northeastern shore of Brazil. There a new portal has formed and is blossoming now, to channel new understandings and a new quality into life on earth. You are part of that expression. In the ways that count most that is your spiritual home.

Gabriela asked not only about her life purpose, she also chose the word "mission." We all come with a purpose, but few come with a mission. She also asked to be helped to affect collective consciousness and the planet too. Few seekers ask such big questions. What came in answer was also bold in scale, and of course, given to be used over many years, a lifetime in fact.

She was introduced to the concept of a "portal," an idea with which she was not familiar. A portal can be seen as a foothold on earth for a wave of souls, a birthplace with its own unique wavelengths that cannot be separated from the purpose for which the portal was created. These wavelengths support the soul and form a foundation to the personality. These portals are prepared over ages, not for a few, but for many. A portal is a big subject and we'll look at it again later in this book.

And what else do we see? The healing practice that will occupy most of your life will be a face to face practice, not one to one, but done in small groups, families, and small communities. Your vibration, your ability to inspire trust and love, practiced face to face, will be the carrier wave that opens doors in consciousness for those who will read what you write. You will not depend on media appearances or worldwide fame to attract to yourself those who most need to hear what you have to give. Your message will be conveyed to those almost exclusively younger, even much younger than you, and it will blossom as those souls come to adulthood. You are in it for the long haul, Gabriela.

That was conveyed on a high and symbolic plane! Do you have questions about any of it?

Gabriela: Could you be more specific?

Brian: There are energies in this portal. There is a reason why Miami has become the working capital of Latin America. Those energies and that city are vibrant, alive, bursting with new life and new ideas. Miami is far and away the most vibrant city on this continent.

Know that the wave of immigration from all of Latin America into the southern parts of the United States is the most life-giving and important wave of change that this continent is experiencing at this time. And that will be true for your entire life. It's taking different forms in Los Angeles, in Phoenix, in Tucson, Houston, Dallas, Tampa, Miami, and the near cities of the southern border. Each of those communities has a different vibration and each is drawing a different population.

You will be shaped in the near future by your visits to Latin America and the Caribbean. That's all we'll say about that at this time, but these things are vitally important to you. You have been genetically encoded to apprehend these changes.

Gabriela had certainly experienced her life's journey as rich with meaning. She respected her own choices, but she had not glimpsed the larger, almost public, dimension given here. She had pursued personal growth and spiritual practices and personal growth, meaning to support radiant health and become a whole person. Gabriela's second question, which she had also prepared in advance, was a question I often hear from body-workers and massage therapists:

Gabriela: Where and why is my energy blocked at this time in my life? How can I dissolve these blocks? Do I know at some level rituals, traditions, or practices to dissolve these? Please reference former lives if that is wise.

Brian: We have a huge volume here. Let's look first at your energy body. We see first the link between the heart and the lungs, the link that's called the cardio-respiratory center, immediately beneath the sternum. Yours was specially designed by you before you came here, not to be unique in your generation, but it's a pioneer design, honestly.

You have great courage. That's written in this heart, written in the spleen and the kidneys and the liver, which all support the heart.

But you also have respiratory vulnerability. Your lungs will require your mindful and informed care until you reach the second half of your life. Pay attention to the atmosphere where you live and work. You are more vulnerable than most to air pollution.

Cigarette smoke especially is poison to you. Your body resembles the bodies of infants and very young children who are coming into this life now, more vulnerable in the lungs, able to take this risk because they'll be grow up in a world where cigarette smoke has been largely banished. That's not true of the world you live in, but nevertheless you've got the lungs those children will have. Do those yogas which emphasize the breath. Make them your own without fear and without tension. You came to do it.

Now, the usual language of "blocks," which generally refers to emotional blocks, needs some updating, Gabriela. Blocks are not blocks at all. They are carefully designed limitations placed in your emotional body to require you to grow in your own path at the pace that is right for you. When you exceed that pace or make a wrong turn, your respiratory system will announce its distress. Do you understand? That's where your symptoms will appear, but that's not a block: that's your protection.

Now, does that heart energy flow freely through your circulatory and respiratory systems? Not as freely as you might like. You have, in addition to a courageous heart, a fearless mind. That's not always a good thing, Gabriela. Your mind might take you in over your head, might take you where you had best not go. Your lungs and your heart together will announce when you're on dangerous ground. Those are not blocks, they are more like the fuses in an automobile engine. They will fail when overloaded, understand?

What else do we see? The blocks about the heart are not about selfishness at all. Selfishness is not your issue. A tendency to burn the candle at both ends, a tendency to work to exhaustion for unselfish reasons: those are your issues, Gabriela. Does this ring true?

Gabriela: Yes.

Brian: All right. Be mindful! You have a long life ahead and a lot to do. Remember that those who need you most are going to be quite young when you first meet them. Much of what you have to give is not for your own generation, but for its children. And some you'll meet as young adults, almost a full generation from now. Pace yourself, so that you are still energetic and vital when you meet them.

What else do we see now in this emotional body? We are seeing the pelvis, or more properly, the lowest parts of the lumbar spine. They are vulnerable in your body, as they are in every body. When you have the consciousness that violence is near and your survival is threatened, this lower lumbar spine will make problems for you. The first remedy for you will be meditation.

Your question in those meditations should be, "What threat do I perceive, to my survival, to my very being?" You have, let us say, in the lessons of your life, some people … some are family members, some are not … who will sound notes in your life that will cause you to feel at risk. Seriously, endangered. At that time, when those feelings occur, when your lumbar spine begins to report pain and ache, that is not arthritis. Those are soul memories. They announce themselves when you encounter the people who have brought you low, even to death, in other lives. There are some of those people in your life, and some you have some yet to meet. Do you understand?

Gabriela: Yes.

Brian: Not everyone in your life, or in your family, is as unselfish or as conscious of the planet as you are. Some of them, through selfishness and some of them through what we must call "dedication to abrupt and violent action," can threaten you. This is not a passing worry. These events when they occur will cause you to wonder if you're going to survive.

You are going to survive. What you need to do in those moments is withdraw into yourself, and remember why you came. And remember that you too are an immortal soul, and none of these things, even these things that threaten the body, actually threaten you.

One of the lessons in your life is to extend the fearlessness of your mind into your solar plexus. That is the place where such emotions are housed. You need to overcome those fears by truly experiencing, over and over, in your meditations and in your prayers, that you are an immortal being who cannot be harmed. Nor can your purpose be threatened by any other human being. Is that clear?

Gabriela: Yes.

Brian: It is not simply misfortune that some of the people in your family life have a tendency to violence. That lesson is there for a reason. Let's look at a life or two and see what we see. First, we see the helmet of a *conquistador*. Do you know that word?

Gabriela: No.

Brian: We see the helmet worn by those soldiers who came out from Spain in the 16th and 17th centuries to conquer Latin America. Not simply with the horse and the sword and the cannon, but by turning the indigenous populations against each other, for those Spanish armies primarily attracted tens of thousands of what we would call Indian followers, and sent them to war against other great cities of South America.

You had not one, but two lives in that setting. In one life you were a conquistador. Not a long life, for you did die valiantly in those combats. And a second life, as what we would today call a Peruvian, although there was no such word as "Peru" in that time. He was a victim of the conquistadors, an unselfish man, a leader, one responsible for his people. He saw the Spanish threat clearly and he tried over a long life to turn it back. He died believing that he had failed. The echo of this death gives you a vulnerability to discouragement.

There are threats that you will meet in this life which you will perceive as threatening the extinction of your people. You will know fear when you encounter these challenges. Go then in prayer to the Source of your being, to those decisions you made before you came here, and you will learn, you will hear, you will be reinforced. You will not die valiantly in this life, nor will your people be extinguished, and you will be so guided.

You will have that protection and that guidance because you will undertake responsibility for young and vulnerable people, who will not have the money, the forces, or the social networks to defend themselves against some of the more powerful groups who will array themselves against the people that you love.

Gabriela: I would like a little more clarification on that.

Brian: You will love and serve people who will be seen as unimportant minorities, as you have been seen. You will love and serve people who will be seen as outside the mainstream, and as always in this time and every other time, society in the mass, the forces that accrue great amounts of money, the forces that send armies abroad, will array themselves against such people, including those you love and serve. But they will not be extinguished while you guide them.

Gabriela: Yes.

Brian: This is not about social class. It's not really about race, whatever that is. It's not about country of origin. It's really about a stream of humanity, a stream whose dedication to the earth, to agriculture, to the sea and the products of the sea, and to a simpler way of life, will make them vulnerable for most of your lifetime. Vulnerable to great money, great companies and, how can we put this? To governments who are accustomed to enforcing their will with soldiers. Does that make sense to you?

Gabriela: Yes, it does.

Brian: Don't be afraid. You will be guided and protected when that day comes. You've seen it coming, but it has not yet touched your soul. It will, though, before you leave this life. And when these conflicts come into your life you will perceive them as quite threatening to those you love.

Gabriela had another question, also prepared in advance: "How and why does fear enter in here?"

Brian: Of course, we've just answered some of that. Like most souls, as you prepared between lives for this one, you did have a preview of what's coming to your generation. Only parts of that preview have come to mind because you've grown up in a North American culture, but your stream of life covers both of the Americas, and it's new.

What you've learned in North American culture, what you've been taught in school, what you have read -- this won't be news to you – will not be adequate for you to put your ideas into words. The fear that you feel is that when you need it, you won't have the words, you won't have the eloquence it takes to guide, and warn, and shape the generation you are responsible for.

When that happens, Gabriela, think of the egret, rare and beautiful, flying just far enough above the earth to be safe from arrows. You are an egret, and as an egret, you must fly above these conflicts, and be admired. And like the egret, your message will be both perceived and received as a beautiful message. Your fear is that you will fall to earth, that you will lack the eloquence, the words, and the ideas necessary to uphold that generation you have taken responsibility for.

Gabriela, that is not possible. Remember that. Others may fall, others whose equipment and mission is different, others in the very stream of life you've entered to be a part of. You will not fall.

Keep in your life those who value your way of knowing and your way of being and you will always be supported, not lonely, but borne up instead. I know that's a big generality. Use your heart and your wisdom to keep those people close to you and to recognize them when they enter your life. It is important. You did not come into this life to experience Dark Nights of the Soul. Do you know that phrase?

Gabriela: Yes.

Brian: You came instead to truly sail through and above the hard times, like the egret. Keep in your life those who value that quality, and the support will be there. You earned that kind of support in that life in Peru. That was an unselfish, patient life, where years and years of courage and endurance were required of you. You earned the right to a life lit by grace this time. Does that language make sense to you?"

Gabriela: Yes. And I think that all of this gives me clarity about a lot of things that were questions in my mind --- things that I have been feeling, I guess. Honestly, I would just be open to know if there's any other information that it's important for me to know right now.

Brian: That's just the question we always close with, what else could or should be given at this time? Just a moment.

Well, Gabriela, I'm seeing an old-fashioned typewriter, and I mean really old-fashioned: black painted metal, a manual typewriter of course. It's a symbol here.

Gabriela, start writing. In time, your voice will take form and shape, but start writing now. Keep a journal. Write letters to friends and save your letters, and what you say is more important than what they write back to you. Build the habit of expressing in writing what you care about most. That old typewriter says to me and to you, "You won't find this so easy or expeditious at this point in your life." Have you been a writer?

Gabriela: Yes.

Brian: Well, you have an instrument to build. Build it. It will build slowly and steadily, and it will be a few years before you glimpse your own power, your own voice and your own message, but start now. Open that channel and keep it open. You need to know that. This is not just another piece of advice. It's important to your health at this time. Do you understand?

Gabriela: Yes.

Brian: All right. Let's speak no more threats or warnings. Do that writing! It won't necessarily feel good. It won't necessarily satisfy you or scratch the itch. Do it anyway.

That's a blessing, Gabriela. When you sit down to write, take a moment. Close your eyes. Put your fingers on the keyboard. You're not alone. Sense those who are with you. Some of them will be entities much like us, souls. Some of them will be other entities we barely have language for. They are the archetypes of your stream of life, too big for words, too big for names. You are learning to channel what they have to give the earth, through your gift of language. They will be there. With that blessing, we are through for now.

Gabriela's is one of more than a dozen readings done in the last ten years that include a prophecy regarding the future of Brazil and the near parts of the Caribbean. Like the other predictions that occasionally appear in these readings, this one was called up for one woman for whom it would be relevant and important. Not as a digression, but as a necessary detail that would matter more and more as she lived out her life. Also in this 2018 reading and others, and particularly important to Gabriela, there are predictions of an epidemic and racial oppression that will blossom as that epidemic inspires fear and unrest throughout society.

That same prophetic dimension also marks the information regarding the respiratory vulnerability of the generation which includes Gabriela's own child, only two years old at the time of the reading. Finally, there is advice here for every channel who is taking, or will take, responsibility for a soul family and a great purpose.

For this reason, Gabriela, some of your most perplexing lessons will not be personal. They will be forged in spirit to raise up the qualities and mature understanding you will need to serve your mission.

So we are shaped, even in our private times of meditation and prayer, prepared to meet the challenges of our generation and our destinies. These things are not personal and we are equipped to rise above them by our own integrity.

Given in Florida June 2018
Gabriela was on the phone from Texas

Wendy and the Seventh Inning Stretch

Chapter 13

I HAD KNOWN WENDY FOR MANY YEARS when she asked for a reading. Although we had scattered after our years in the Fellowship, we stayed in touch over time. I knew her to be a musician with gifts as a leader of song, and I knew her to be an organizer and an activist too. She had learned and taught Paul Solomon's material and made it her own. And she had been at least equally committed to the teachings of The Course in Miracles, material I did not know well.

I also knew her as a special educator and as the mother of a handicapped child. I loved to visit her and her husband because their relationship to that child was probably the most beautiful I have ever encountered. I often wished I could have somehow exported that to the families of the handicapped children that I worked with, and I guess through telling some of the family stories, I did a little bit.

She came for a reading as her seventieth birthday drew near. Despite that number, when she stands up to lead a song or give a talk the years disappear. Really I still can't picture her as an older person, because she continues to be energetic and totally present in every situation. But age and the leftovers of some diseases have told a bit and we dealt with those things.

Sharon, the conductor here, says: Consider the talents and gifts of this life as planned and as lived. Be present with us as needed, you witnesses, you servants of the Christ Spirit, you Masters of this Fellowship too. Convey to us, please the Record of Wendy ---------------, born _________, 1948, in Brussels, Belgium.

Brian: This Record has a cover today, white, gleaming, shiny -- something alive, almost like a perfect piano key. Underneath it is a thick book, for this is a soul who came to cover a lot of ground. Choral music issues forth from this record without words, but with voices that trade places and make harmonies and rhythms that are quite lovely. With that as a theme, let's proceed to the questions.

The conductor asks Wendy's first question: What is the best way to serve The One in these times, to use the best of my skills and abilities? A, Conflict Resolution, B, Game and travel, C, Terminal Diagnosis Project, or D, other?

Brian: The Masters aren't often given multiple choice questions with spelled out answers, and they're laughing! All right … the most wonderful talents asked for and richly given in this life aren't on this list. For this woman asked to be utterly responsive to the emotions of people in front of her, and utterly responsive too to her own emotions, which have been rich and at times even overwhelming.

She asked for that so she could feel the emotions of everyone in front of her: adults, children, even strangers. She fashioned herself a perfect instrument. The strings of her instrument are her own emotions, of course, and her soul experiences, which have resonated quite close to consciousness for Wendy throughout her life. If there has been confusion about this, the confusion can be summed up this way: "These emotions that I'm feeling, I don't recognize them!" But rarely has she thought to say, "Are these mine?"

They often were not, because as people have come before her, people she's prepared to help, their emotions arrive before they do. They play sympathetic chords in Wendy's being. That's been a lifelong condition. That is not a lack of integrity. That is utter integrity to the task she set about herself.

She did come to share joy. She also came to make people strong. And oh, the anger that sometimes flares, and the impatience that never quite disappears, were also asked for, because she often has ignited the fire in sleepy or downtrodden or discouraged souls, and so a fire lives in Wendy to this day. It is not a character defect.

That anger is the second great gift you asked for. And yes, when you look at the nation and the world, sometimes the anger, the suffering, the injustice, and mostly, the *meanness* overwhelm you, Wendy. Then you struggle to find the way and the place and the people upon whom to spend these energies, which have been released in your being, again and again and again, and will be until the day you leave this body behind.

Know too that you didn't ask for the gift of serenity. You have it, but you built it. Do you understand that, Wendy?

Wendy: Yes.

Brian: You built it over and over from life's lessons. You transmuted those lessons into serenity and acceptance, although you only found words for this when someone in front of you needed to hear them. It was sharing that was always meant to be the path: sharing in many settings, with many different populations, and sometimes, different purposes. Sharing to heal, sharing to lift up, sharing to make strong, sharing to give people what they need to confront what in their lives needs confronting. These have been your gifts.

Your reasoning mind, having made an inventory of your skills, your toolbox, and of the opportunities that beckon, would like some concrete answers here. In truth, if you wanted, all the opportunities you have listed could be, if embraced, everything you want them to be. The only hazard would be spreading yourself thin and exhausting this body.

Wendy hasn't always listened to this body and its warning signs. Wendy, who stirs up what needs to be stirred up in others, has never found for long the ability to so quiet herself that she isn't restless for the next opportunity to share her gifts. That's not bad, that's the person you designed yourself to be. Hard on yourself often, hard on others sometimes. There is nothing so extraordinary in either of those dimensions.

Wendy has made of herself a public servant. She meant to be that. In her lifetime, the public roles most often assigned to her were for a person who sees herself as a teacher, as a musician, as a leader, even as a voice in the wilderness, calling out for those who can't find their own voices. Of course she's been all of these things.

What she hasn't been is a person who can stand up and say, "I'm a certified, fully trained, totally prepared, such and such" – because what you have prepared yourself to be is a rich and generous soul. And you have been that.

I don't know if you know this language, but it's being given: Wendy, you've reached the point where it's time for the seventh inning stretch. Do you know that phrase?

Wendy: Yes.

Brian: All right. Don't be in a hurry to grab hold of the next task. Your gifts will not go away, nor are you so specialized that you must find the one perfect opportunity to give what you have to give. You broadcast your being when it's time to sway another or a roomful of others. That's what your voice was designed to do, and it does that. The emotions that fill you are perfect for the situation at hand. Of course, you can be impatient for results, but in a moment, those people who have heard you begin to stir, and begin to fashion their own results and solutions.

Then you have done what you came to do, do you understand? You set fire to the light within. You were born to ignite souls. You've done it all your life. Now, what have I not addressed in that first question as Wendy wrote it?

Conductor: Specifically, Conflict Resolution, the Game, and the Terminal Diagnosis Project. Can you comment on any of those specifics?

Brian: Conflict resolution: you've learned those skills. Conflict resolution is not about getting people to forgive each other. More often, it's about shaking them up and pointing them in a direction they haven't seen before. You do this supremely well. You make conflicts resolve. Honestly, you *make* them resolve. You come like a knight on a horse. Sometimes people resolve their conflicts to get out of your way, do you understand? That's how you meant for it to be. You do it very well.

Now, "The Game." You've been responsible to this gift. Oh, my.

It'll continue to grow and spread. It would continue to grow and spread if you left this planet tomorrow, but you enjoy it, and who knows which soul in front of you will embrace this game and carry it forward and apply it, in places you'll never see and never hear of? Some have already been chosen, Wendy, and as long as you do this work, more will be chosen. Is it necessary to have a glossy board, perfectly printed? An utterly comprehensive set of Game cards? It isn't really necessary. It is the input and the love of the person who guides The Game in each circle --- that's the real Game, and it works.

Now let us look closely at the Terminal Diagnosis Project. Is that the term you used?

Wendy: Yes.

We're having a change of cast here, because you have attracted to yourself some Masters who will help people. They will also introduce concepts that are not currently employed in the dialogues about this phase of the soul's life. These concepts were not imprinted on you, they are concepts that you've not heard with your own earthly ears. These are concepts you will give voice to.

You have had a first-class graduate education in the end of life. You know vastly more than you think you know. You know because you've walked through it and not given up. You know because you have taken in these experiences and integrated them in a wordless way. You'll hear yourself saying things you've never heard or read on earth. New concepts, new tools, for a new generation who won't be dying as our generation dies, nor as our parents' generation died.

Death has not always been the same on this earth, not at all. The range of ways that humans have died is vastly, vastly beyond our reach intellectually, because of the beliefs that have vanished, because of the cultures and the systems that have vanished, because of the many, many changes that have occupied the waves of souls who have entered this earth, done their work, and departed, leaving no historical record for us to absorb.

How does the indigenous person die on her own island, drawing in her gods from the earth beneath her feet, from the sea in which she swam, from the spirits that came when she danced? We barely know that answer. But you know it.

You've done the dances, walked on that earth, and swum in that ocean. Who will come to you needing to die that way? Those who have been pushed out of their islands. Those who have been required by life to bathe in different oceans. Those who have forgotten what they learned as infants in their mother's womb. Those who have lost the dances that give life.

You can channel all of these things. You can channel them just as well for that New York native to whom every one of these things – soil, ocean and the spirit of dance – are utter and complete strangers. You can devise protocols that you can teach others, so they too can channel their own soul knowledge to the dying one.

There isn't one way to die. There isn't a way sanctified alone by the Ancient Wisdom as the best way.

We have the Egyptian Book of the Dead but it's not so useful anymore. Souls have come in wave after wave with different orientations and different soul knowledge. In this society at this time most have probably learned more at the movies than at grandmother's knee. This is true because death is hidden away and whispered about. We've lost the understandings that permit us to walk into that passage prepared and unafraid, strong in the traditions we've made our own.

You will give people their traditions. You will draw them out of your soul in its dialogue with their souls, and you are equipped to train others to do exactly the same thing. There isn't one way. There are thousands and thousands.

Go ahead with your study. You'll learn what you need to know from the people you teach. That's been the model in this Fellowship! You understand that, I know. What's our next question?"

The Conductor reads Wendy's prepared question: How does a person or a soul leave the body? Be specific, including body activities, mental activities, and spiritual practices.

Brian: First a spirit draws near, whether to a person unfamiliar with their own spirit, or to a person who senses that the spirit will conduct them safely to an unfamiliar place. Fear, discomfort … these are the feelings that spirits approach first in what we might think of as a natural or a normal death. We prepare for two, three, four years. We prepare as different thoughts come into our minds. We prepare as images come to the surface of consciousness. We prepare as childhood memories announce themselves, sometimes in dream, sometimes in reverie, sometimes in talking with our dearest friends.

It is not necessary to interpret or understand these things. It's only necessary to relax and dwell in them. That's the most important part of the dying person's preparation for death, to spend that time in dialogue with memories, with souls who have gone on, with experiences that touched the soul in ways that person never found words for.

This you evoke. First you make that person safe in your presence. How do we make strangers safe as we lead them into a meditative state? We share our laughter, our confidence, we open up our bellies and surround these people with support. That's task one.

We radiate to them that we are not afraid of death, that we're at home in these passages. They hear that. They hear it almost regardless of what words you use. As you take a hand, and their eyes meet yours and they see no fear there, their own soul experience will stand up and assert itself, saying, "I'm in the right hands now. This person knows this journey I'm on, and she is confident of my arrival in the next place."

What gets in the way here? Of course, inadequate teachings, religious dogma, other experiences of that soul, deaths that were not natural, not harmonious, not prepared for. We do store the vibrations of any abrupt or violent death that we witness. They come back in those moments.

When the middle schooler is killed in a car accident and you sit in the classroom with her classmates, what are they processing? Their own traumas, their own abrupt, inadequately processed blows. It's not different for the dying person.

So you listen, and the things that they say frequently make no sense, or they are so profound that you can hardly dialogue with them as we all move gradually onto the other plane.

Some people elect to abandon cognition and let dementia or Alzheimer's take them away gradually. Others choose to have a stroke and lie quietly for weeks or months, then leave the way a bird flies out a newly opened window. Still other people say, "I'll have one last lesson, thank you. I'll fight and kick and wrestle and struggle to understand." They've chosen that way, and so you sit with them and the whole message is, "I'm here." No other message is required. Still other people have made a plan, and your job is to intuit that plan and support it. Yes, those are the rare ones, but aren't they a joy?

You already understand all of these things. You may not have words for them yet. But you've faced them. You've lost a child. There is no wound deeper. You've seen your mother through a difficult death and you've recovered. You know those two outcomes.

There are other kinds of deaths. In other cultures, people are sung out of the body. It's very natural. In some cultures, people leave the body to music from instruments -- equally natural. Truly fortunate people leave the body accompanied by bird song, or by the sounds of ocean waves, or by the household sounds of a busy family, rattling dishes in the kitchen while children laugh in another room. These are all very good ways to leave the body, focused on the wonder of those events, not focused on fears or questions. So Wendy, be open in that minute to what's around you, because it has always been prepared.

It isn't your job to prepare it. Every death is a love story. You're a facilitator, do you understand? You will, if you don't now.

Conductor: Wendy has been diagnosed with calcium loss and it has become both persistent and painful. She has had other diseases in the course of her life but this one has lingered on without changing much. It seems to resist her efforts to understand and correct it.

Brian: Let's begin with stress. You've been parent and caregiver to a child with developmental handicaps. We don't know a surer recipe for long-term stress. You've met those challenges wonderfully. You've found and kept a partner who supported you in that task. That was a gift!

But there's been pain, and some of it lingers, not in your mind, nor even in your emotions. It's in your body, and you need to heal this body with your body's senses, all right? With a hot tub, with scented body wash, with blossoms floating on the water. You need to lie with your eyes closed in a tidal pool and listen to seagulls call. You need to stand on that mountaintop, listening to the trees down below as they brush each other and make love to the air. You need to let your body really be there. Don't take your watch or your phone. Let your body wisdom assert itself.

Now, what should you be consuming? What is your body equipped to pull calcium from, in the form you need it?

Plantains first. Lightly baked, emphasis lightly! Or lightly fried.

Mixed with a catalyst that plantains love, like black eyed peas, like mild red peppers, or ginger. Plantains first, several times a week. Don't think about your waistline. The pain and the calcium losses are more important. What else?

Grape juice. Even commercial grape juice. Grapes and grape leaves are rich in calcium. That's why the Greeks eat them. Have grape juice every day.

Conductor: Skin, any other health issues, including liver growths?

Brian: All right, including liver growths, if we have them. We'll start with the liver.

You have only encysted tumors, and "encysted" means encapsulated. Bodies that heal from cancer rarely eliminate all the cancer. Instead, they encapsulate it with a cancer-proof membrane. We call that a cyst.

Sometimes it's called, if it occurs in the breast, "fibrous tumors." Those are actually encapsulated cancers too. We all have them from middle life and beyond.

That is what you have in your liver. Your liver is not, at this point, vulnerable to the ordinary kinds of liver disease. It has suffered in the past and it is bigger than your body originally designed it to be, because those parts of the liver that have grown hard and inactive are still there, well nourished by blood, and that's not unusual. We see a fundamentally healthy liver and a liver that has benefited very much from your willingness to exercise the lower half of your body in all the ways that you do. That includes dance, and that includes your vigorous walk, which is more than a style. It's a very healthy adaptation. Above all, it includes the enthusiasm with which you throw yourself into things. You race towards the next idea. That habit of mind benefits your entire body.

Let's look elsewhere in this body. A general scan, not in detail … okay, you have scar tissue through the ears, of course, from your surgeries. We see them through the jaws and up even into the temporal lobes. You have scar tissue in various places from intravenous injections into intravenous ports. None of this scar tissue is greatly affecting your health, but it's a challenge for your heart to overcome these narrowed spaces, and now we are talking about both arterial and venous circulation. What can be done in a systemic way?

What I'm given first is rose hips, and I'm given that word before I'm given vitamin C. There's really no plant on Earth having more naturally and fully accessible vitamin C than rose hips. Grow them in your garden. Pick them off beach roses when you can find them. Steep them in water in the sunlight for two or three days. Drink some of that tea every day, not one cup but two or three. It will greatly improve your circulation by principles and processes that medicine is still trying hard not to see, but if you've not read Linus Pauling on vitamin C, read him and know that his speculations are every bit as valuable as his research. The man understood vitamin C.

Not as a capsule, not as a pill, not as a supplement, but the living vitamin C with its wavelengths alive and intact. That will correct your circulation problems. Those problems stem from narrowed veins and arteries, and scar tissue too. Some of those scars are widely distributed. Let's look at the great vessels of the heart, because that's where we fear these things.

All right, the great vessels of the heart are *ductile*. They expand and contract with the beating of the heart. Yours, as in every person over the age of 50, aren't as motile as they once were. What can you do about that? You can quite literally massage the muscles of your chest and around your heart and in your abdomen, because the heart depends very much on energy from the solar plexus, released upward to the heart by laughter, by good emotions in the company of loved ones; and of course by exercise, exercise that is so much fun that you're laughing out loud when you do it.

Feed your heart with that exercise and those relaxing factors, and you'll do the best that can be done to overcome some of the weaknesses in the great vessels of your heart. Do you have frank heart disease? What you have is a precursor, and you may live with that precursor thirty years if you take care of this heart. Is it going to rise up and strike you down in the foreseeable future? No, but take care of it.

Dispel, drag into the sunlight, and discard all fears. No one who has a heart diagnosis in the offing is free of fear. No one. Do you understand what was just said?

Wendy: I think so.

Conductor: Is there anything else that could be or should be given at this time?

Brian: Wendy, you are loved. You are supported. Most of your mistakes are corrected before you make them. That's the kind of guidance that you've earned in this life, and that's the kind of listening you have done, and yes, our teacher is part of that picture. Others are too, including other teachers, other bands in spirit, and other esoteric lodges. Your own history with that way of understanding life is long, it's always been available to you, and you've used it very well. That's been a blessing.

If you ever question yourself because your language sounds less learned, because your utterances are short, pithy and heartfelt, instead of long and sophisticated when you draw on that knowledge, count that as a gift, do you understand? You convey esoteric knowledge in language that works very well around the kitchen table.

Try to hear this: it has never led you astray. What you think of as your mistakes were in fact your lessons, designed by you and agreed to, before you came here. Don't judge your life by anyone else's standards. You have lived the life you designed for yourself to live. You've had some hard lessons. You've drawn wisdom and love and compassion from them. You'll continue to do it. That's a blessing and promise, and with that, we are through for now.

Given in Virginia Beach
May 2017
Conducted by Sharon Solomon
Wendy was present

Anna, a Writer and a Priestess

Chapter 14

ANNA AT FIFTY IS CONSCIOUSLY LIVING OUT the role of a priestess in waking up the souls who come to her. As you will see, her diplomas and her profession were only passages necessary for her to become what she is now, and we have no modern word for what she is now. Her contemporary labels and the roles they point to do not represent at all what she has to give. When we met she said to me, "I am a healer but I can't describe what I do."

I had not met Anna before she appeared at the Fellowship of the Inner Light for a reading. The impression she made from the first few minutes was one of extraordinary integrity, plus dedication to this path she has undertaken. As I write this I cannot really remember her face, or how she was clothed, or what she may have said in the way of small talk before the reading began. But the impression of her strength and her love is with me as if it happened this morning, indelible and exciting.

Sarah, the Conductor here: Source of our beings, select what we see, and guide our understanding as you convey to us please the Book of Life for _________, now known as Anna ________, born ----1961, in ------------------------. Today is December ----, 2014.

Brian: All right, we have this record, and its cover is dark stone, almost like jade. This seems to be Latin American in origin, carved in glyphs and ornamented in what appears to have been molten gold, poured into grooves worked in figures around the face of this book. Taken together, this is an emblem of truly ancient wisdom that has been transformed, not just through modern life, but through quite a few lives, represented here by the gold. The blend of these life streams -- because truly they are life streams, not cultures -- has resulted in an inner knowing. It's hard to categorize, hard to label, but it was prepared for that part of the life yet to be lived. We'll have more to say about that. Let's proceed to the questions.

Conductor: Please give guidance as to how Anna can launch her healing practice.

Brian: Well, this won't go away. First, we see a quill pen, and let's unfold this symbol.

Anna has within her -- let's not call it a book, but instead, a body of written work, actually prepared in another life, actually published in another life; and waiting to simply be rewritten in English with a few adjustments for a modern audience.

Not prose so much as discourse, to be written out as prose, but to have the feeling and the purposes and instrumentation of speech, one-to-one. This is not a genre that's easy to describe. It is meant not to call but to summon, those who have themselves prepared over time in many cases before coming here to receive what she has to give. So that what she writes really will be a series of letters to souls that are her friends, from whom she has been temporarily apart. Letters addressed in the first person to one or two -- frankly, women -- at a time. A story of consciousness, a story more of wholeness and of healing. And very much a story of empowerment, very much the promise to be conveyed to those of her sisters not only trying to come awake, but trying to come awake and cover the ground that she herself has covered this time, and not simply in a feminist sense.

Women, mothers particularly, can speak of creation from the knowledge in their bodies. This is not a collection of concepts arrogantly put. It is more nearly a series of impressions. The same impressions that you would write to your dearest friends, left on a continent far behind you, to persuade them to come over. Very personal, very direct, and not needing to have the kinds of tidy chapter headings and neat summations that we usually expect in what we call nonfiction writing.

You mean to write of your dearest and most private experiences, and not to draw conclusions, lessons, or maxims. But instead to convey them as you felt them. And to convey the life they gave you as you lived through them and overcame. You won power. Yes, lit by love, but power, nonetheless, and that's what you need to convey in writing. Write these things, look about you for the opportunity to distribute them. Publication is not so important in the sense of a book, as distribution is important. Ideally, distribution through gatherings, workshops and conferences where you will sometimes speak and sometimes be in the audience, with a supply of your writing with you. Anna, do you understand?

Anna: Yes.

Brian: All right. It should not be seen as a barrier or a mountain to climb. These things are complete within you, not channeled. This is your experience, your gifts to give your sisters and their daughters, do you understand?

Anna: Yes.

Brian: All right. It is enough to say, "This is the ground I walked on, this is what I experienced, and this that I've given you is the music and the poetry that was left in the wake of that experience." So that first, and it won't be hard to do.

Now, to go to those conferences, carry your volumes, show them, speak up as you have learned to do. To say deliberately, "I have answers for you. I can find your answers for you, in your body, in your consciousness, in what will pass between us. We call it healing. But I can help you become whole, with my glance, my touch, with the fields of energy that I will emanate as we draw close." And those fields of energy will activate your kindred fields of energy, not even chakra to chakra, but being to being. You will see your sisters, not as people with issues in their bodies or personalities to make stronger or more complete, but as beings coming into their own to manifest their wholeness on earth. Do you understand?

Anna: Yes.

Brian: All right. You'll find the words to say these things, to look another woman in the eye and speak plainly. A lot of words won't be required because once you have their attention, the transmission will be complete, sometimes without words. They will come to you for healing. As in ancient temples, men, but more often women, and mostly by tradition expectant mothers, came to particular temples. They didn't expect to be instructed, they didn't expect to be fed such and such a diet or do such and such exercises. They came to be blessed by a priestess, charged and empowered by heavenly forces able to give that kind of wholeness to women. That's what you really are. Do you understand that?

Anna: Yes.

Brian: All right. This has very little to do with licenses, certification or training. This has to do with your long work. You've been making a home in your body, in your life and in your being for your ancient knowledge, and that process is complete. It will grow. It will change as you learn from the beings you work on, but it is complete now.

Travel to those conferences, speak in the lobby, in the sharing times, in the rooms after the evening has ended. Just go with a sense of expectancy and when another woman speaks, what you need to say to her, the words you need to begin with will be given. You don't have to prepare a pitch or a spiel. It will be unique each time. It'll be eye to eye, touch to touch. You do have to put yourself forward. Are you ready?

Anna: I am.

Brian: Good. Then not a lot more needs to be said about how to begin, and how to -- not charge exactly, but how to convey to them what of their substance they need to hand to you, frankly in order to receive the gift you will give them. Place your hands upon them and say, "What I'm going to give to you will unfold over the next phase of your life. I may give it in five minutes, or I may give it in two hours. It's valuable. It's certainly two hundred dollars worth of value, or more, but give what you can." And most will give more. Do you understand?

Anna: I do.

Brian: Can you do it?

Anna: I will.

Brian: Good, because, yes, in order to be practical, in order to carry on, in order to invest this time, you must be adequately recompensed for what you give. And yes, it will feel great in the giving, but times of rest and recovery will be required. It's an energy transmission, you see. You'll need to be quiet and let those who have worked with you, and prepared you since before you were born, recharge and rebuild your batteries uniquely, for the next set of encounters, for it won't always be the same. Do you understand?

Anna: I do.

Brian: There is a team in spirit and you are the quarterback on earth. It's not even appropriate to say who is senior and who is junior. It isn't like that, it is reciprocal. If you want a label for those in spirit we suggest they are "the forces becoming," and some will be spirits who have been humans, and some will be entities. However, the best word for what the others will be is archetypal forces; but you will be face to face with them. They will speak through your vocal chords. They will be transmitted through your presence. Do you understand?

Anna: I do.

Brian: All right. Is there a contemporary label for what you do? Healing is close enough for now, and vague enough that they won't know what to expect, and that's good. Because they will look into your eyes and say "Lead me, touch me, give life to these mysteries.'" That is what you want them to feel. Do you have a question about that?

Anna: No.

Brian: There will be some men. There'll even be some teenage males! Nothing in their words or demeanor will reveal to you what's going on in their souls. Don't worry about it. The spiritual teachers for the next thirty to forty years will be women. They won't be called reverend or doctor or professor or guru or guide. You're one of those.

Souls have been prepared, not to recognize exactly, but to feel themselves drawn to you and your sisters in this work. Even those young males will be drawn. They won't know why, they may say things that are inappropriate, but you have lived with that at home, haven't you? You won't be fazed, you'll recognize that stuff. You'll brush it aside, and not by accident have you lived with that at home, because many of those who come to you are going to be twenty and under. Do you understand?

Anna: I do.

Brian: Well they certainly won't have words for what they're looking for and that's the way it should be. All right, Sara. Let's move on to the next question.

Conductor, reading the next question: Anna would like to know the reasons that she feels an affinity for, and a pull, to Brazil and Peru.

Brian: I have a change of cast now. Some of these faces have features this channel has never seen before. They are not from another planet but they are alien to this time. It's been a long, long time since they've been on earth in bodies of flesh. That's some of them. Some of them have been with you in former lives, as humans, like you. Some of them have dwelt forever and timelessly in spirit. How should we describe them? Eternally youthful, if you can understand this, Anna.

Anna: Mm-mm.

Brian: They are like the spirit who comes to take us when it's time to cross over, for those servants too are impossibly youthful and energetic in appearance. Have you seen them?

Anna: I have.

Brian: All right. You will not be aiding the work of those who help individuals to cross over. But these -- I'm going to call them angels -- understand that sometimes tremendous new growth involves experiences that feel a lot like death, to those who let go of what they have believed to be their lives. You'll bring them through that. You'll bring them through that because they'll look at you and say, "She knows what is happening here, and she must know the way to the other shore." Do you understand?

Anna: I do.

Brian: All right. You yourself asked for and received a kind of strength such that you never looked at death in this life, and said, "I'm ready, get me out of here. This is too hard."

No. Stubborn is not exactly the word, but when things got tough, your real inclination was to seek shelter, and from shelter, spit those opposing forces in the eye! That quality is strength, and those less strong will borrow yours to make the changes they need to make.

One cannot live in a corrosive, modern, conventional home, and turn around and introduce the light and grow into it in that same home. It wasn't possible for you. It won't be possible for those who come to you. That doesn't mean you'll be the Angel of Divorce. It does mean you'll support women who make unthinkable changes. Do you understand?

Anna: No, I don't.

Brian: They are going to be women who grew up being told that they needed to get degrees and graduate degrees, that they needed to be certified as teachers, healers, doctors. They are going to be women who had been told, "You must be a mother," or, "There are rules for whom you can love," and you're going to tell them there's no guide to these issues but the inner guide. There's no path to follow but the one that's written in your soul. It may seem scary to them, it may seem to them like heady irresponsibility, but you are not an irresponsible person, nor are you giddy. They will look at you and know that what you're helping them move into is not wild and crazy. Now, do you understand?

Anna: Yes.

Brian: All right. Because you yourself are a rock. You probably don't think of yourself that way, but you are, and that's how they will see you. Tender at times, funny, approachable, but not to be put off or deterred, no.

Now, coming back to Peru, coming back to Brazil, these lands once supported great, sophisticated societies, sophisticated beyond the ability of anthropologists to ken or to grasp, given what remains. That society depended upon the sea for protein, for commerce, for profit, for worship. This may be hard to grasp, but they worked the sea, and dwelt for long periods in the highest mountains. They built systems of tunnels and canals and roads which will come to light in the next thirty years. They will be found. They do survive. No one suspects their existence at this time. They have been protected.

They will be found and made public. They will be made famous. There will be a flood tide of wild conjecture about how they were used and what those lives were like. And it'll be a hundred years before anything like an accurate picture will be available to the public. That does not matter, and it's not your job to describe it truly. It is your job to tend to the young who will find their way there, breathe in these values, take them from the sea, take them from the shores, take them from the mountain tops, and bring them back to their homes on every continent, and begin to live those ancient values. They will do it despite the languages they speak, despite the governments they live under, despite what they've learned in their schools.

Your job is to find them and help them step into the unknown.

That unknown is broadcasting like a series of beacons along a line that starts on the western coast of South America and crosses the

Andes, headed northeast to Brazil. As the relics of the saints of every religion were once placed beneath cathedrals and crypts and pagodas to broadcast signals from the sky into the earth, to make the land bright, so these ancient artifacts scattered along that line are broadcasting signals through the earth and into the atmosphere to draw those souls who are entering to live this way.

All of that will come out of your mouth one tiny bit at a time. You won't paint the grand picture or write the coffee table book. What you will do is help the women and the young who come to you saying, "Something is trying to be born." And you will help them give birth to it. And it's their words that will dress this experience so they can carry it forward. You'll draw it forth but it won't be your words they carry forth. Do you understand?

Anna: I do.

Brian: All right. Those tunnels … those tunnels originate on the coast of Chile, and Peru, and what once was the coast of Bolivia, travel in a northeast line under the Andes, and go to the northeast corner of Brazil. In ancient times they proceeded on to what we call Atlantis. The very last and best part of Atlantis to sink beneath sea was on that same axis in the Caribbean, in the Atlantic, northeast of Brazil. For us to describe here how all that was programmed into the earth exceeds the abilities of this channel, and far exceeds the time we have to work.

The pyramids in the Maya Country, those mysterious stone structures in the highest ranges of the Andes, and the tunnels themselves, speak to those who go there. Their secrets will never be revealed to the archaeologists, the scientists, the historians. That history is lost forever but the energy has only been dormant. It is necessary to travel there. It is necessary to walk that earth, climb those heights, stand with your feet in those waters on both coasts, to apprehend and make that energy your own. There are pilgrimages required of you. Do you understand?

Anna: I do.

Brian: All right. What you receive there will not come to your mouth or your mind in words, but it will come out of your mouth and your hands and your being, as you heal one by one the sons and daughters of this portal. Do you understand?

Anna: I do.

Brian: All right. Goodness these are grand terms! You'll be all your life doing this. There'll be times when you forget all of these things as you support, wrestle, pray for, the people who come to you. There will be times when you will rack your brains to say to that woman who's sinking under the difficulties of change, "This is bigger than you think it is, love."

You need to go ahead. You'll never be quite alive if you do not. I think you understand that. That's where your consciousness will be, and you'll be with them one, two, five at a time. And you will work hard. So will they. You will never be sorry that you did it. And their children will fashion societies, and structures, and ways of life, we just cannot picture; any more than the Spaniards who landed on that continent and the northern Europeans who landed on this continent could possibly have foreseen what this continent and its peoples would become. We are talking about change and growth of the same magnitude.

It will be built largely on those South American soils, but it will be exported in units so small, that it'll be a dozen souls in loosely organized units who will, as our generation did, seek out healthy food and clean water, and make new music. They'll work through what it takes to shrug off the old forms and raise their children by laws and rules and principles that have not yet found words. But you will see that.

You'll even see it here on this coast in this time on earth. It has begun here. The pilgrims are going, and they're coming back again, and they're going back and coming back again. They're going back to the western coast of North America, they're going back to Europe, they're going back to the northern rim of the Mediterranean. They're going back to the northern coasts of the British Isles. They're going back, if you can believe it, to the far western coast of northern Africa. These cells are in place, they've begun to grow.

You may be able to visit them. They won't be in the headlines, they won't have slick four-color brochures, but they'll be there. Some of them will come to the A.R.E. just as they come now to Findhorn and what's this mountain, this mountain in the west, Mount Shasta?

Anna: Yes.

Brian: To the hills of northern Thailand and northern Burma, to Indonesia and Malaysia and to India. These cells are in place. There are the centers, the spiritual centers, which have grown up and flourished.

They have taken what we call the New Age and turned them into living communities. They don't much resemble what they started with, but they are as they should be, and doing what they're supposed to be doing. People are finding them. And they'll go on from there to visit Chile, Bolivia, Peru, Columbia, and return home again. You're a part of that. You may not get to go there very often, you may not get to stay long. But it's a change in your being you're going to experience. And it's written in that soil and in that sand, and it's in the living waters of those coasts. You'll receive it, you know how. Do you have a question about that?

Anna: No.

Brian: All right. Sara, what do we have next?

Conductor: our next question is, what previous lifetimes would it be helpful to know about in light of what Anna is living now?

Brian: This will surprise you. I'm seeing a sword not made of metal. Made of a substance … let's see if we can get this word ... it isn't schist, it isn't glass, it's volcanic in origin like steatite. The Maya, the Inca, the Olmec made weapons of it.

Conductor: Obsidian?

Brian: Perhaps. Brittle, but if chipped properly, sharper than any modern razor. They were cut into simple blades. They were also cut into highly elaborate symbolic shapes, such as the ones mounted on staffs that you carried as a priest, not of the Inca, not of the Aztecs, but of an older people. Four times, we see, you lived that life, four times in cities … let's see, this word is not democracy.

You established and maintained and contributed to the government of cities where *economic justice* prevailed, where trade was far and wide with the entire known world. Where astrologer-priests and philosopher-kings took part in the councils of government, and truly devoted themselves to living at peace, though they were surrounded by warring city-states.

You have worked many times to create wise governments. This time you'll use that knowledge, that confidence in front of a crowd, to create the citizens who will populate the states and cities they will build that will have those qualities. Do you understand?

Anna: Not sure.

Brian: You can't read this in a history book. Okay, I'm being corrected. In the book called *1491*, by Charles Mann, you will read how the philosophers who staffed the courts of the Inca kings tried to reason with their Spanish conquerors. Now, the philosophies they had mastered, though decayed from their highest point, were recorded in the Codexes.

And the Codexes, of course, were prompts from which to channel. They were not written in language. They were like the original hieroglyphics, which had no grammatic structure. Those images were prompts from which to channel, as surely as you could channel by regarding a star, a crystal, a geometric motif, or a Mayan calendar. They can't be translated. They are living entities, and it takes a channel to recite what's recorded there and not recorded in language.

That is described in recent history books. *1491*, I see, is one of those books. Now that was a great society -- in long decline -- but still magnificent, and so recorded by those few Spaniards able to see what was in front of them in the last decades before they utterly destroyed it. Do you understand?

Anna: I do.

Brian: All right. If you read that material it will comfort you. You won't learn there what you're going to learn inside, and what you're going to learn from the beings of the women you work on. But you will be comforted to see that reflection. It's no more alive than are the accounts of Native American beliefs we have today, so diminished from what they truly were when they were living creeds. You understand that I'm sure.

Anna: Yes.

Brian: We try to help indigenous peoples survive and preserve. It's a compassionate effort and worth doing. But for the survival of what they lived and stood for, unnecessary; because infants incarnate knowing. And they work it out as best as they can in the environments they find themselves in. The very lucky few, and the very well-prepared few, become teachers of those values. But oh, my, what a distance they have to travel to turn those soul memories into something conventional contemporary people will come and take part in. Do you understand that?

Anna: I do.

Brian: All right.

Conductor: We're at 10 minutes.

Brian: And that's not your job this time. Your job is to free the women, the younger ones, to pursue their paths, to follow their souls, yes, to Brazil and Peru, and to Mt. Shasta and to Findhorn, and to Angkor Wat. To wake up there, and come home, and alter their lives and their directions. You'll help them do that.

And they will form the communities, bear the children who will be born more fully prepared, facing less resistance, than will the young women you work on, do you understand?

Anna: I do.

Brian: Okay. You'll be working on two, three, four, five generations. There will be one woman in front of you but literally, many generations of souls attending, and frankly, helping you help that woman manifest what's trying to be born, even as Edgar Cayce played with his invisible imaginary friends as a preschooler. When he told those stories, the most liberal-minded of his family thought he was talking about fairies and imaginary friends. But no, he was playing with his colleagues before they were born. With Gladys Davis, with Hugh Lynn, with his cousins and his in-laws, with Gertrude. They were his company when he was a preschooler and the first of that team to incarnate.

You'll be assisting the first of the team to stand up on their feet and grow and be whole, and those who will be born to them will be there in the room, helping, making jokes, and playing with you. You will perceive them. And they won't be, oh, Native Americans, or the spirits that live in the grove near the house where you happen to be. They will be the team you're clearing the way for. Do you understand?

Anna: I do.

Brian: You've reached far into the past and you'll be reaching far into the future. And all of that will quicken your senses and sustain you, because we as ordinary humans need that kind of excitement to go on. And so you'll be aided to see as much as you can stand to see, and it won't be difficult. Sara, what remains?

Conductor: We had discussed what attitudes are her strengths and what attitudes are her hindrances.

Brian: We've covered some of that.

Conductor: Yes, we have.

Brian: Let's talk about your hindrances … oh, sometimes there's a feeling that you have to let your anger show a little in order to say what you have to say. Try hard to let the strength show, and let the anger, which is an ego expression, diminish. Do you understand?

Anna: I do.

Brian: All right. It will go better with the people close to you. That's where it hinders sometimes, that's where it cost you sometimes, let's put it that way. Look at those you love as your allies chosen by God. They have no concepts to give you. They don't have much help to give you, but they do love you. If you can accept their love exactly as they offer it, you'll be sustained by it. Try to release your expectations of them. Try to accept the love they give in exactly the form in which it's offered. They're doing their best, do you understand?

Anna: I do.

Brian: All right. And don't be afraid ever to give love back in exactly the way it comes to your mind, your tongue, your hands and your body. Do you understand?

Anna: I do.

Brian: All right, it will take you places you've never been before, but that's to be looked forward to.

Other attitudes? The medical profession is utterly irrelevant to what you do. And if from time to time you are questioned, or frankly, threats are made: shrug it off. You'll be protected as you sail under the radar and do that which not only you are not licensed to do, but which no one else is licensed to do. Do you understand?

Anna: I do.

Brian: All right. You're not a therapist, you're not a counselor, you're not a psychiatrist or a physician. You are one who makes whole. Honestly, you're a priestess, and nobody is licensing priestesses! You will be protected by those who protect priestesses, and they have always been protected. That's a promise and a blessing and with that we're through for now.

Anna: Thank you.

Given in Virginia Beach, Virginia
December, 2014
Conducted by Sarah Anderson
Anna was present

Cassie, a Healer in the Mountains

Chapter 15

CASSIE CONDUCTED HER OWN reading in the sanctuary of the Fellowship of the Inner Light in Virginia Beach. She had long ago mastered the Terraces and the Temple, the meditations of Inner Light Consciousness. She guided me through the meadow, up the terraced mountain, and into the temple at the summit. She took me into the Hall of Records in that temple. There she asked that I be given her Book of Life, the Akashic Record of her own soul. It was a wonderful experience for me to make that journey guided so surely by someone who had truly made it her own.

Cassie: Do you have the book of life for Cassie ____?
Brian: Yes. It's being handed to me by a robed figure, and one whom I rarely see. He's gazing into my eyes. I have the book by the bottom. He holds it by the top. And he releases it to me, having conveyed to me a seriousness unique in my experience in these readings.
The book itself … it's not right to call this a cover. The front of the

book is a gold and white damask material. There's an oval window in the center. There is a golden braid around the edges, not all the way out to the edges, but set in a little. That golden braid is gathered in figures at the corners of the rectangle. And now in the oval, we see Cassie, dressed in identical robes to the figure that handed me this book, with a golden – don't know the word for this garment -- a gold-worked vestment over her shoulders and down her neck. This is the garment of her priesthood, which is beyond gender, for in this expression, this expression of her wholeness, she is beyond gender.

And now the image in the book dissolves into light. And we're seeing the ages roll by. Starting in the Egypt of the Pharaohs and going further back, back to a simpler, more modest Egypt. Back to that land referred to as "The City of the Hills and Plains." Back to the Aryan Kingdom in Central Asia, in the foothills of the Himalayas. Back to a civilization for which we have no word in English, a civilization that followed on the heels of Atlantis, and occupied the shores of the Asian continent where the China Sea is now. Back to Atlantis, and back further to a time on earth when the entities sang with the morning stars, and used the powers of their minds to complete the creation of earth and make it a suitable habitation for humans.

There is a long, long, ensoulment here with many other chapters, too numerous to list. But in this existence, she is ready to fully express the timelessness of the stream that populates this planet, and inhabits – there's no good word for this – the environs, the atmosphere about this planet, which in truth is not like a layer of gas. But is a finer energy that interpenetrates earth life and earth substance, and animates and directs creation.

It is in this element that what we call the soul, what we would call Cassie's soul – although that word is not adequate to this identity – it's in this finer element that Cassie is at home in her work on earth.

It's not simply light, although it is certainly full of light. It's irradiation. It has the properties of radiation, and is dedicated, among other things, to the formation and revision of DNA. Not just human DNA, but the DNA of all living creatures. Dedicated as well, if you can picture this, to the revisioning of nature's forms: earth forms, trees and vegetation, animal life, the life of the elemental forces, the atmosphere, the tides; even the starlight.

All of this is a serious challenge to this channel's vocabulary. These are not concepts. These are forces, forces with which Cassie is entirely at home. And though for most of this life she has been animated by and expressed these forces, they elude a language for her, too.

These forces have occupied, entered, and expressed through her being in every setting, and in every imaginable way. And having then done their work, here and there from time to time, released -- grip is not the word -- released the *receptors* in her body to other forces of a similar nature. So that Cassie's identity as a personality has been too fluid, too changeful to pin down. Or, we would have to say, too fluid to comfort Cassie, the woman, as she made her way on earth, and in a life, and made a home on earth for the person that she is, with earthly structures to fill out and perform. Cassie, does this make sense to you?

Cassie: Yes, it does.

Brian: All right. In many ways you have been a person and an entity animated by the wind. Winds of force and energy that have passed through you, permeated you, and then passed on and been transmitted to others. But that hasn't made it easy for you to say, "this is who and what I am." You feel it. You know it. But we don't have words for it.

That's what you really have been, what you really are and shall be, and when this body is used up, you'll find yourself once again at home in this entity, so much like a shower of light, so much like a breeze, so much a life-giving force: not needful of a bodily home. It has been necessary to master this body, to master this three, and too, the fourth, and the fifth dimensional world, to function. That's been a puzzle at times!

Cassie: Yes, it has.

Brian: You have at times experienced that as imperatives to function here and function there in climes where you did not feel at home! That is no defect in you. This earth is in flux. This earth is still growing and changing and becoming. This earth is a planet with a destiny still unfolding, whose nature, whose vibration, whose physics is and are still being built and formed according to purposes not yet seen by humanity. You have felt these things and you have felt these forces, but you have looked in vain for the language, movements, and ideas that expressed adequately what you feel. Do you understand that?

Cassie: No, I don't. Is there more clarification that can be had?

Brian: Let's see what we can do. You too, have been a person dedicated to making whole, but making whole according to new orders, new kinds of births, new beginnings. You have seen healing as a matter of body, mind and spirit. But making whole has two more dimensions.

Body, mind, and spirit are able to operate and are created in harmony with that which is becoming, which is larger than mankind. That is one additional dimension. To say it is a group effort would be wholly inadequate. It's a huge effort. Every soul on earth and every guiding entity about the earth is part of that effort.

The other dimension is hard to find words for. It's composed of energy entering into time. Energy fashioning itself to flow into the lives of men and women, children, and souls at their earth-conception. Energy – we would probably say today, programmed – loaded with the ideas they will live out over their entire lives.

You've been aware of those streams that animated the Native American expression, probably more keenly aware of that stream than any other. You've also been influenced by, but less aware of, those streams that have flowed through this portal and others, wearing the costumes and the concepts of ancient Egypt. And you've been aware of what we call the Masters. The Masters too, wear concepts when they appear, costumes really, when they appear in the minds and the imaginations of men and women. It's easy to think that, for example, the Order of Melchizedek is adequately expressed by robes and orbs and light, but that is simply its earthly costume.

It is as modern as tomorrow. It's aims and purposes and projects are written in increments of fifty, a hundred, and two hundred years, reaching forward; and tens of thousands of years reaching back. It's not adequate to say, "That's progress."

But progress is one face of it, progress that makes earth more habitable, progress that makes earth more fit to support and nourish humans as they build societies that are kind, loving, and supportive. Cassie, the woman, understands that. Cassie, the woman, understands how important it has been, and is, to nourish what in our society raises up lovers of peace, adults devoted to the love of children, lovers of that which erases disease and suffering. You see? We're avoiding that word "healing" because we think we know what healing is. Truly, we don't.

That which erases disease and suffering -- that's one face of healing. That which reconciles, that pours into humans what we call the elements and streams and energies of former lives, and that's a true thing. It's quite hard for us to see, but it's equally composed of elements and streams and energies of future lives. Every life builds future lives. Every life resolves and makes whole former lives. Do you understand that?

Cassie: Yes.

Brian: All right. Not uniquely on earth at this time, but certainly only a few are able to apprehend and transmit those energies. That has been your path.

Sometimes you have felt a compound of awe and fear in giving what you have to give. All because, to tell the truth -- despite the overworked nature of the word -- these energies are indeed awesome, vast. And fear due to the lingering thought that you might not be adequate, that you might repeat what you tend to see as your mistakes in former lives.

Again and again you have undertaken to introduce into human life the pioneering energies, and often undertaken to introduce those energies in situations not adequate to apprehend and ensoul them. Do you understand? You have a great tendency to bite off very big chunks! Do you understand that?

Cassie: Oh, yes.

Brian: All right. No fault to you. No harm. If you could, you would hold every soul in your arms as tenderly as a mother holds an infant. That is your mainspring in this life. Whew! That's hard to do on earth, very hard to do. Souls come in as eager as teenagers to get on with it. They don't want to regress, even for a moment, to that infant-like state they frankly enjoyed as they prepared to come for a given incarnation. It doesn't feel good to an eager soul to wait to engage with its life and its personality. Oh, my, you would hold them for twenty and thirty years at a time until they were safe to proceed. Do you understand?

Cassie: (laughing) Yes.

Brian: Okay. No fault. There's no fault in this. It's your mainspring. You are, truly, a daughter of Isis. You truly understand the Great Mother, the Virgin Mary, Hathor. These energies are not strangers to you. And you have transmitted these things. You've looked for the visible signs that these energies have been received. But of course it takes, twenty, thirty, and forty years for the out-workings of what you give to be perceptible to human eyes. Do you understand?

Cassie: Yes.

Brian: All right. You feed souls for the long run and you have fed hundreds. Be proud! You have done what you came to do. You're still doing it. You'll go on doing it. But put on the vestments, the chasuble, the raiment of the priestess. Stand tall. Let go of the fear that it might not be received, that you might fail. It's time to let go of that fear.

Time to let go of that which sometimes restricts your throat, which is heard almost ... almost as a kind of speech disorder, like those that speech therapists work with in young children. Truly in those young children those in-coordinations in the muscles, in the organs of speech, reflect the inability of those young bodies to speak and sing the songs they know they have to sing. Do you understand?

Cassie: Yes, I do.

Brian: All right. Look closely at the young children who need speech therapy. They are the singers of earth, the singers of earth's new songs. Now in your own life and your own work at this time let's look at that and try to come down to street level.

This won't go away. We are seeing the mountains of Virginia. We are seeing souls that flock there to support each other and be nourished, in part, by teachers or, more truly, by each other. They come for instruction and gathering and fellowship. That is your most natural arena to teach and share and heal. Do you understand?

Cassie: Yes.

Brian: All right. That is your home on earth, in this body. There you can hear unimpeded the voices that animated the Native Americans, that kept this earth in blossom for thousands of years. And hear as well the voices of that which they kept in blossom, having fed the trees, the flowers, the streams and even the stones. It is as important to you as you think it is. And there is a world yet to be given from those forces, not necessarily or even mostly in the language, the rituals, the symbols, and the images of Native America.

Directly, Cassie, by your touch it will be given. When you let your eyes meet one to whom that you have something to give, you will, for a few seconds, a few minutes, or a few hours, lift up their souls, and hold them to your breast as mother holds a baby. You will transmit what you have to give. Do you understand?

Cassie: Yes. Am I to understand that my place is in the mountains, rather than the shore, where I have recently settled?

Brian: Your teaching place is in the mountains.

Cassie: Oh. I understand that.

Brian: Your home is on the shore --

Cassie: Yes.

-- you have fashioned to support you, to be the place of rest and fellowship with your friends. Keep it. Go to the mountains and teach and share, and come back to your home to renew your earthly body and your earthly ties. Do you see?

Cassie: Yes. That makes perfect sense. Thank you.

Your body would suffer if you resided in the mountains. For you, the downloads would never stop. You could kiss sleep goodbye if you lived in the mountains! That's not good for your body or any other body. Go there, share, drink the cup and pass it on, and come home again. Make your own meals. Sleep in your own bed. See your friends. The sea that laps these shores renews you.

Cassie: It does.

Brian: You are utterly connected to this portal, and the true nature of this portal is the sea pouring energy into this land. And let's not tie that up with civilizations, cultures, or symbol systems. The sea itself sustains and renews you. Let's leave it at that. Not just the water, but the tides and the sea breezes. Oh my! And the joyful company of the ocean birds, all of those things. This is your home on earth. Your teaching home is in the mountains. We would say, your temple is in the mountains but your home is here. Not the temple where you worship and meditate, but the temple where you meet the seekers who want and need the healing, and the spark, and the lift forward. That's in the mountains. Is that clear, what we've done so far?

Cassie: Yes, and it feels right. It's affirmation, confirmation, and I've been quite a while assembling the mountain sanctuary and making contacts there.

Brian: You've been quite a while assembling this home too, and it's there for you. When we think of the ancient priests and priestesses, we forget how many were wandering saints. Yes, the three wise men live in the legend, the Magi; but there was a whole class of Magi in ancient times. Their locus was centered in Bible times in what we now call Persia, and before that in what we now think of as the Northwest reaches of India, Nepal and Tibet. Oh my, they traveled far and they traveled on every continent!

They had other homes. Truly their homes have always been high above the plains, above the shoreline, for all the reasons you already know, up where the air is clear and the stars are close.

I am seeing the Andes, the great mountains of Mongolia and Tibet, even the Urals in Central Europe, and in the mountains that plunge down to the sea in Scandinavia. And the mountains that rise off the sea floor in Hawaii, as well. The Verdean Islands off the coast of Western Africa too, and the mountains that appear as tiny atolls in the far Pacific. Those are mountains. Their bottoms are on the sea floor, but if you measure their height from the sea floor, they are taller than the Himalayas. Do you understand?

Cassie: Hmm. I do.

Brian: All right. They are very important places. They may not be impressive to human eyes, but it is there that the Masters meet ... well, we want to say, their favorite students ... and bring them along, as they take their places, which is not a single, final step. They rise and teach beside the Masters for a time, and then return to their earthly homes. And come back later and do the same thing again. They teach beside the masters as these Inner Light Consciousness persons taught beside their Master Teacher. And then they either leave or are cast out into the street, to renew their earthly homes and renew their earthly ministries. And yes, to meet their earthly lessons.

For those who came to this Fellowship, and for those who learned from this Master Teacher – and he was a Master Teacher – those transitions were made as gentle as they could be fashioned. Do you understand?

Cassie: Yes.

Brian: This Fellowship draws travelers! It doesn't draw the people who settle in and wait for the gold watch and the pension. They don't come here. The Fellowship's members go back and forth from the heights to the streets, and they serve, all of them. It may not always be apparent to the human eyes but they really do. And they really always have.

And the fruit of that effort is truly not yet apparent. It will be apparent in the next one hundred to two hundred years as their work blossoms fully in the beings and the lives of children and grandchildren and infants not yet born, for whom this portal was the energy that opened the doors and made ready the earth to receive the seed. Do you understand?

Cassie: Yes.

Brian: That's a long process! This Fellowship was not founded in 1972. It was old in 1492. Do you understand?

Cassie: Yes, yes.

Brian: Okay. This is just the latest incarnation. Oh, the New World was prepared a very long time for its job on this planet in this time! The great and sophisticated civilizations that have flourished here, and vanished without an archaeological trace! Their story has never been told. And the evidence is gone. Oh my, this earth's surface has changed and changed and changed again.

The geologists cannot read the Record. They can read the antiquity of it. But the structures that supported human life and progress -- they vanish when earth changes come. We have been through quite a few cycles of earth changes.

You can think in those terms. This is not news to you. You have never been hung up on the need to find the evidence in the last 10,000 years. That's way too small a span to see how things have begun, and grown, and disappeared and returned. Hundreds and hundreds of thousands of years is the appropriate span. Do you understand?

Cassie: Yes.

Brian: All right. Although the evidences will be found in the sea floor, have been found already in this century, it would be understatement to say, "They've not been recognized for what they are." They don't look like what we expect the evidence of civilization to look like.

Most of what has been found in this part of the world has been found in Mexico, and not recognized. It will continue to be found in the Andes Mountains. Not in the Amazon basin, which was an inland sea, but on the eastern coast of South America, and in those islands whose mountaintops form the islands of the Caribbean now, which once were a chain of mountains that extended all the way to the mouth of the Mediterranean. This was a very long time ago, when you could call the continent Pangea. Do you know that name?

Cassie: I've heard of it.

Brian: All right. Not so important now what it was called, but yes, it was home to Atlantis. And yes, it had its counterpart in the Pacific waters north of Guam. Their presence is unsuspected by geologists, but that doesn't matter. They live in spirit. They've never stopped doing their work.

Even at this moment, honestly, this body can hardly cope with the energies that are trying for expression here. They're big. They're not inhuman, but contemporary humans can't really apprehend and express them without long conditioning. This channel's body is meeting energies here with which it has not been familiar. Do you understand?

Cassie: Yes. I've been working with beings of light from Lemuria.

Brian: Yes. Yes, you have. They give you a cheery hello!

Cassie: I should say they've been working with me.

Brian: That's mutual. You are not their subordinate, you know. You're a partner. It is reciprocal.

We haven't the faintest notion of what that society was like. We haven't had, for the last 10,000 years or so, languages which had the words to express what that stream of humanity -- it wasn't a culture -- lived.

It's coming back, but it won't resemble its ancient forms; but it will do the same work that Lemuria did. Of Atlantis, we have only touched the very tip of what it has to give. It will give what it has to give. It will be giving it for about four hundred years. That's what it will take to apprehend and express it. Oh, can we find a word for that?

Cassie: We have ten more minutes!

Brian: All right. Yes, the Atlanteans mastered what we think of as radio and electricity, and other wave forms too. We're aware of them in crystals. We're beginning to become aware of how they work when those crystals are excited by polarized energies.

But that wasn't their greatest gift. Their greatest gift was the ability to rest between lives without having to reincarnate, and return and return and return and return until they became, we would say, so socially skilled that they could cooperate at a level we cannot conceive. That's the real gift of Atlantis. If we're going to create world peace -- and we are! -- that's what we'll draw on to do it. Do you understand?

Cassie: The energies of those Atlanteans . . .

Brian: Atlantis. Yes …

Cassie: Ooh, yes.

… their energies and their understandings, and we too, if you can believe it, will begin to have inconceivably long lives. Although in the beginning these individuals will have to disappear to rest and regenerate. They'll change their names when they come back because it will be a little uncomfortable for others. Do you understand?

Cassie: Yes.

Brian: That's been happening right along. The Masters have done that right along. Shambhala is a place of rest and regeneration. It is not inhabited by what we think of as spirits. Do you understand?

Cassie: It's inhabited by human bodies?

Brian: It's inhabited by human consciousnesses …

Cassie: Oh!

Brian: … able to fashion bodies to do the work they need to do, and then retreat to Shambhala with those bodies, and rest those bodies. When they reappear they don't look like they appeared the last time they walked to do their work. Do you understand?

Cassie: Yes. Thank you.

Brian: All right. Do they walk among us? They surely do. Do they identify themselves? Never! It'd be too distracting. All right. Are they Avatars? That's not the word. Oh, Lord this channel doesn't have a word for what they are. Elder Brothers has to serve, and Elder Sisters, by the way. Not locked in gender. Do you understand?

Cassie: Not what?

Brian: Not locked in gender.

Cassie: Oh, yes.

Brian: Gender is irrelevant to what they do.

Cassie: Yes.

Brian: Now, before we proceed to what else could be given, what questions have come to mind for you? If any?

Cassie: Under what modality, what guise, will I be offering teachings in the mountains? I am understanding that I'm really radiating energy to people, but there will be a modality that they expect they come to me for?

Brian: They expect to receive Native American style healing from you. Which you're quite capable to transmit.

Cassie: Oh, okay.

Brian: All right. They expect you to be that wise old woman in the woods. You fashioned a body that's a fit for the role, do you understand? All right. You didn't come to have Kim Novak's body.

Cassie: No!

Brian: You've got a perfect body for what you're led to do. That's what they expect you to be. You can play that role and enjoy it. It's natural to you. You've been that a number of times, in both male and female guise.

It's just not the limit of what you're giving. You'll heal bodies. You'll heal their beings. You'll help them give birth to the new lives latent in their incarnations. And I do mean, lives that resemble and are made up from parts or previous incarnations, but will emerge in their expressions as new life. I don't think you have a problem understanding that, if we don't get caught in the words.

Cassie: Very interesting, yes. I do understand that.

Brian: All right. It wouldn't be bad for you to wear skirts when you do this work, and loose-fitting tops, and necklaces made of materials like turquoise, shell, agate, coral. Understand?

Cassie: Yes.

Brian: The vibration will be right for what they've come for. More than metal, better than metal. Just a passing note.

Cassie: Yes. I have that clothing and jewelry.

Brian: Of course you do! Wear it in the mountains when you work. As far as the world is concerned, you'll be a spiritual healer, healing by touch. Helping them solve the personal problems we all think we have, only in reality, those problems aren't personal at all. They are the healing plan. Every symptom is a blessing – I think you understand that already.

Cassie: Yes.

Brian: Now, what more could or should be given to you at this time? … you did not ask for eloquence in this incarnation. Oh, what is this quality? It is tied into your loving, unthreatened, approving gaze, which you turn on those you heal. It is tied into the mother love, which, candidly, flows from your breasts more than from your hands. It depends on your ability, if you can understand it, to transform the ground upon which you stand to holy ground, in the moment it's needed. When a person draws close to you physically for a hug or to hold hands, you transform the ground upon which you stand to holy ground. Do you understand?

Cassie: I do.

Brian: And you can feel it, too.

Cassie: I do.

Brian: Energy flowing in and out. Not like alternating current, but like circular patterns of energy passing through you. You asked for that gift and you have it. Even though it's not well known in this time, you transform that ground, by the way. Yes, your feet are a blessing upon the mountains like the feet of the prophets. Do you know that phrase?

Cassie: No, I don't.

Brian: "How beautiful on the mountains are the feet of him who brings good tidings.'" That's how it's put in both the Old and the New Testament. It refers to a real physics that does occur, and you have that physics to give. It's your gift.

All your learning permits you to stand unthreatened in the face of any story the people tell you. You will not judge. You will neither approve nor disapprove. You know very well that your ministry is to souls, not to persons. You are not fazed by tangled lives and expensive mistakes. That's not your job. Your job is to kiss the soul and give it life. Whatever words you need will be given, and they will be adapted to each seeker. And you just give them without doubt. You don't need to quote books or direct people to pamphlets. You will send them to the places where their healings can be made lasting because the environment is right. What awaits them there is usually not well labeled, but it's real. You have that blessing to give, too.

You will stand with your back straight, your feet solidly planted on earth. And the more you give the more your body will be made youthful. Any and every complaint in that body will be healed and will vanish. Do you understand?

Cassie: Yes.

Brian: You will have a perfect grip on your health into advanced years because you do this work. You will be, not preserved, but made young every time you do it. What a blessing that is.

Cassie: Oh, my gosh!

Brian: And your mind will remain clear into advanced years. Don't fear the years as they mount. That's a blessing.

Oh, we've only been able to give a small fraction of what there is for you, but you have the means to bring the rest into your body and into your being, as you have done for years. Change in your spiritual practices is not required.

More and more what you have sought in meditation will be given to you in the moment you share it in healing. You'll know it. You'll be fed, richly. That is blessing and a promise and if you could see---maybe you do see -- the legion of beings that has shaped and supported and trained you in this work, and they will go on doing it---this building could not contain them. That's a blessing. Oh, reluctantly, with that blessing we are through for now.

Cassie: And I am grateful.

Given in Virginia Beach
January 2015
Cassie conducted her own reading

Leora and the Spirit of Inner Light Consciousness

Chapter 16

LEORA WAS AN INNER LIGHT CONSCIOUSNESS GUIDE who was present in the early days of the Fellowship of the Inner Light, when Paul and his I.L.C. Guides traveled the world. This writer was one too. In those days there was a steady stream of visitors to the little church in Virginia Beach, people who had come to taste the Mystery School. They often stayed for weeks and months. The energy was high and the day-to-day was tumultuous, for who knew what a Mystery School was supposed to be like?

To those of us who lived it in those early days, it was a dizzying round of instruction, long hours, hectic days, lessons and miracles. Trips across North America and foreign continents were a constant. An extraordinary stream of teachers, personal experiences, healings and dramatic comings and goings were also a part of it.

Leora asks, may I invoke the presence of the band of spirits that were with Inner Light Consciousness in the 1970's? If so, how do I do it? If not, what changes do I need to make for that to be possible?

Brian: These entities, who are spirits, Universal Forces, and Angelic

Ones, are ever eager to come where hearts are aflame with love for an immanent God.

Those who have long supped with the Christ burn with a steady and an even flame. And indeed, love radiates from them, as from a steady source. This is the Middle Way.

But the thirst for God grows intense in those who have lost the way, and fallen, those who long to be released. For the thirst for the presence of God is not far from the longing to be released from this body and return to the stars. Where are the thirsty ones, the hungry ones? The ones with the pent-up love, long denied?

They're in the party houses by the beach. They're in the homes where violence, profanity, and anger have made a prison of the homestead. They're in the streets, living there, on fire with desire. Yes, they know that. But the image in their minds is alcohol, drugs, sexual ecstasy, a place to hide … and adventure.

Do not troll the streets. But promise the adventure. Because falling in love with God is a great adventure. Promise the miracle. Dig until you have the stories to tell. Tell your own stories. These people are easier to bring in the door than they are to manage once they've arrived. And the many skills which you have mastered will be required to bring them to a steady perch on God's trapeze.

But it is these people, who have spent eighteen, twenty, thirty years on earth, never dreaming that there is a heaven, a real one – *and there is* – never dreaming that the most powerful human instrument there is, is a touch, a loving unselfish touch, delivered by a whole person.

When these discoveries wash over them, the deepest and best memories of the soul are released in a rush. In that moment, the image you hold will determine whether what we have is healing or hysteria. You picture the healings you see they need, whether physical, emotional, or mental. Picture it, hold it. Make those images of wholeness your own. Love these people with a passion, a passion to see them in those scenes walking with the Angels. Believe that it can be done. And in the moment when the dams are burst, you will give form to what is born. More in your presence, your strength and your steadiness, than in the words.

There was a time when most humans saw the gods. Saw them in the night fogs and in the flames of the fire, heard them scream in the hills and the forests, felt them arrive in naked power. And in that day, the spiritual person was the one who saw it, and heard it, and knew it was true, and did not panic. But stood up with human will, and said, "This, this belief and image that I hold like a shield, is what we must do."

And the gods do not obey, but those attracted by that image will come and do what you have visualized. And the other gods will go back to the forests and the mountains and the fields and the darkness.

Yes, see, see your children, because they are not students yet, see your children as rescued souls to be put on their feet and taken up a path that you design. Not by manipulation, not by dogma, not by what we call "teachings." Instead, by the image that fills your eyes and mind and heart when you look at them. See that ragged girl standing tall. See that miserable man laughing. See that liar speaking the truth. No matter what they present to you, you see what you know they can become. And that's what will be given to them through you. Hold it.

You know that you can stand in front of a raging person, and from the steady, strong center of your being, say, "Be still. I love you," and mean it. That's what's needed.

Pray for them and they will come. Their Angels will bring them. Don't go to the shelters. Don't open the door to the desperate who need bedding and a roof and a breakfast. Just pray for those most in need, most ready.

You have read the Gospels. Jesus was not running classes. Jesus ran a walking hospital of the soul. And his prayer was, "Send me the most injured, those closest to the point of collapse inwardly, and I with my strength and my love will open their eyes to what they can be. And we will be whole again together."

This was the spirit of ILC in the seventies. And those who came, came from many places, but they did not come from security, happiness, or health. They came from desperation. A desperation that caused the soul to cry out, "God, come and get me!"

There are never enough to do this work here. The Angels are plentiful but the men and the women are few. It isn't respectable. It doesn't pay well. It is embarrassing, often. And there will be failures.

For every miracle in ILC there was a spectacular failure. It was one to one. But the miracles were real. And can be here, again. Does this congregation want that?

No. They have a steady burning light, and a home. But they are not in this building around the clock. Can you explain, to those appointed to make decisions, that you mean to reignite the fire? Not in the lamp of wisdom … the fire of the sun.

Yes, you can. Expect if you make this prayer that they will come through that door. So too will come those prepared to seek wisdom not in books but in the hearts of the needy. You will have students then. They will not trust you because of your elegant speech or your command of techniques. They will trust you when they see you stand before the raging devil just before he quits the body and the light fills it.

Now, this teacher who declined in health, who founded this Fellowship, had in his experience grown tired … the devil got his coat-tails, that's all.

It does not start with Leora finding a teacher. It starts with Leora's prayer. "Yes, Lord. Put me in harm's way. And I will stand the storm, and love them." And you will. And they will love you back. And you will point to the Christ and say, "That's my strength. Love Him." It can be done. Do you have a question?

Leora: More than I can even fathom.

Brian: It's in there. You know these things. Not perhaps in this life, although you have had your hard walks, but in other lives, you've known that state. You've been the healer, and you've been the lost one too.

You know the tender Angels of art, and child-rearing, and healing. And you have glimpsed the saving Angels, the saving Angels of Michael's army. Yes, they war with the devil, the devil in the lost. And yes, they drive him out. Would they use you? Gratefully. Ponder that.

Leora: How do I stay balanced with that kind of power around me?

Brian: Well … that power will come through you. That's the balance that needs to be found. Because when you invoke such an Angel, you don't sit in the meditative state and watch it work. It fills you. And you become the Ark, and you expend the charge. And then it passes.

Then you're Mrs. ---------- again. And you go home to your husband and your children and your kitchen, and you pray for peace, and do peaceful things. Routine things. And remember, you are Mrs. -----------, and it's Jesus and His angels who do the work, although, in the heat of battle, there is no difference between Leora and Saint Michael. But that passes.

You are not a child. You've given birth to children. You've faced disease. You've seen death. You know that we recover from these things. And you too would recover. Special Tantric techniques are not required to recover stability. Returning to that home you have so long defended – and drawing sustenance from those who love you – that's all that's required.

Do you understand?

Leora: Yes. Thank you. What would I need to do to support these spirits, Angels, Universal Forces, here, For Inner Light Consciousness and the Fellowship?

Brian: Four-fold answer. First, set a schedule. Don't come running when your phone rings. Don't be "The Christ -- Open Around the Clock!" Be here but require them to come to the experience you have scheduled, and to have their crises and their healings here. The Angels will cooperate with you and be grateful. They will gather beforehand, at the appointed hour. They will disperse at the appointed hour. The helper who gives it all, around the clock, is an illusion. So first, schedule.

Two: in this work, in that introductory ILC experience, put away the circle of chairs, and stand up tall. Dress as you would dress if you were called to the front of an auditorium to receive a medal for bravery. Stand up straight. Dress with authority. It's inappropriate in the kitchen, but it's necessary in this kind of ILC.

Ordinary concepts of beauty do not apply. This is not about makeup, or hairstyle, or expensive garments. It's about the right colors, it's about body carriage, it's about gestures which live in your memory.

You have been, in other lives, an orator. You have even been a Senator of Rome when Rome was a Republic. You can look at an audience of any size, and radiate confidence, and remember what you came to do, and do it. Not forgetting that you serve something greater than yourself. As a Senator, you served the Law. You were a male of course. But you believed in the Law, and the Republic. There was no strain of democracy in that republic, but for its place and time, it was true. Sometimes, the curls that turn up around your neck stir faint memories, because that was the Senatorial hair style. When you, as you do at times, don white to enter the Temple, it's a Roman tunic and drape, like a toga or a stola, that you put on.

And what other reservoir of strength can you draw from your Record?

Well -- a Celtic warrior woman, with black armor, trimmed in polished silver. Decisive. Swift, swift to battle; swift to rage. You've felt her. Will you require that warrior woman to use aggression as an Olympic athlete uses aggression, to summon it all, and spend it in the disciplined exercise of the movements memorized through training? You can. Recognize that she was a strong woman. She's in you. You've drawn on her, for good, sometimes not for good.

You are not afraid of the physical challenge. If one of yours was threatened by a wild animal or a moving car, you would summon in an instant what it took to stop the animal, or even the moving car. That's the warrior woman in you. She needs a little polishing for this time and place, but she's in there.

Now we see another life, quite different: a Roman matron of the upper classes, beautiful, slender, tall, olive skin, long straight dark hair. She prayed to Aphrodite. And in her maturity, when that body had thickened, and that hair had grayed, she turned to the Christian message as preached by Paul the Apostle. And she went out from a wealthy home, her fine fabrics covered by a rough woolen shawl, and tended to the sick and the needy, the women in childbirth, even to those wounded in the gladiator combats in the Colosseum. You experienced disgrace among your Patrician friends, and disapproval from your spouse, but you did not ... *did not* leave off from that work. And you died in a state of grace and so earned the opportunity to be here now.

And she too was named Leora. She sold her jewels to fund a ministry. She sheltered the humblest in that beautiful aristocratic home at times, never for long, but when it was really necessary. She earned the love and respect of Christians of every race, because the early Christians were of every race, and every color, and every social strata.

And that early church in Rome, that earliest Christian church in Rome, faced not just ridicule, but murderers, plotters, even those who would throw them in jail, who often succeeded. That church hid at times, fled at times, and reassembled always looking over their shoulders as they went to the place of meeting, to be sure they were not followed.

See for a moment a Rome, not based on military might, as the Roman force abroad was based, but based on a class structure, inviolate, enforced by law and arms. You violated that class structure, and you violated it steadily for many years, until it meant nothing to you. Fear vanished from that Leora's heart.

Yet she remained a woman able to weep, able to nurse, able to inspire confidence and gratitude in people who spoke other languages, who saw her as if she were an empress stepped down from the throne. Because of course, then even more than now, class and wealth were imprinted on your every word and gesture.

They could not be hidden. And you overcame that. And won the right, the opportunity, to have all of those gifts without all the meaningless surface signs attached.

You have the manner, the energy, the ready warmth that is required, and all the other, too. Not a patrician beauty this time. Not a trained creator of elegant banquets. But knowing fully that the beauty of another person is in the heart and the soul, not in the garments, or carriage, or speech, or bearing. And knowing fully that the meal prepared with love and served in time of need is the best banquet.

Express those qualities and some of the drama that has at times inhabited this building will vanish from your experience. It will go on, but it won't touch you. Take your place. Do you understand?

Leora: I'm not exactly sure what you mean by "Take my place."

Brian: Minister. Lead. Heal. Call to yourself those who need what you have to give. More will be added. And needier will be added as you grow in that expression, faster than you may think. See it not as a burden, because it will be a joy. And for you too, an adventure. You'll see miracles, and don't they lift the heart!

So I end this book with one of the earliest readings I have done. It is fiery, different in kind than the others here. But there will be more, another volume already selected, that will soon be ready for print. They too will range from cool to hot and some will sample other dimensions not included here.

That is how it must be, because souls come seeking in far more states than I could ever picture. I appreciate them, not always in the moment, but after time, and I love them, every time. They come with different pasts, different futures, and far different roles.

Given in Virginia Beach
December 2011

Afterword

Is it the point of spiritual life, to do readings? No, not for me. I experience joy when I get to express the best that's in me – but that rarely happens in meditation, or even in prayer. It's not done in solitude. It happens when something inside me which is true connects to something here in the world, or to a face of spirit that I may experience as something other than me.

When all defenses dissolve as I talk with someone, or touch someone; when all separation disappears as I pray for someone; when I forget that I have boundaries and simply flow into music, or dance, or the beauty of the earth before me; in those moments I am one. Not "one with" but really just one, and there is no separation, no self having a perception, completely a part of whatever I regard.

This wholeness is all I really know of healing. Illness, loss, defeat – these things are momentary separations from wholeness. Joy is a part of wholeness, not the other way around.

I do experience this, often, when I do a reading. I perceive the beauty of the life before me, the life of the soul, the inexpressible unity of a family, the wonderful encounters with these old friends. At times I stand once again in another place and time and own every memory and every association there. Remembering the past, remembering the future – there is no difference in these experiences.

Often in a reading I meet someone or something I truly love without reservation. This is like reuniting with my lost and truest love and there are no shadows in that experience. This happens most often when I am reading the Akashic Record. The seeker I read for may be beside me or on a phone in a faraway city. It doesn't matter. The experience for me is the same one. My hope in doing this book is that you, the reader, will experience that connection too.

This more than anything else is why I go on doing readings. I hope I serve those who come. But often, even usually, the realization of a reading is years ahead, even twenty or thirty years ahead. I am not that good a human. If I counted on immediate results readings would be thin nourishment indeed.

I believe the love I experience in this work is not different from the love that blossoms for all of us when we hold a baby, or hear a beautiful melody, or see the ones we love drawing near. I believe it is not different for what overtakes me as I stand on a height and regard Lake Tahoe or I am swallowed up by blazing autumn woods in Connecticut.

Paul Solomon always said he did not remember what he experienced in the reading state. But he did remember, and he did fully appreciate, what occurred when he taught face to face, and entered that same wholeness, as he often did. So it was teaching that meant the most to him. The teaching, the sharing, and the face to face encounters fed him as did little else in life. That was unmistakably clear to those of us who knew him and worked beside him.

Does it only happen for me when I sit, eyes closed, before someone seeking answers? No, it happens often, but after long practice, it happens dependably when I am in the reading situation.

Some seekers are puzzled when I laugh out loud while I am

reading, as I almost always do: it is so joyous. They think they understand when I cry, as I often do. But truly my "sensations" in those two moments are the same ones.

When I teach a person to meditate, it is that joy that I am eager for them to have. Not simply the information, the prescriptions, the learning of the discipline, so like learning to play an instrument! Nor is it only the healing that comes sometimes, although that means a great deal to me. That is so even though their lives will go on, as healings fade into the next ordinary day and the next.

Journal note Panama City, Panama, July 2015